D1044588

THE POWER OF PRAYER

ALSO BY
JONI HILTON:

The Best Kind of Mom

THE POWER OF PRAYER

JONI HILTON

Covenant Communications, Inc.

Cover image by Kim Steele © Photodisc Red Collection/GettyImages.

Cover design copyrighted 2004 by Covenant Communications, Inc.

Published by Covenant Communications, Inc.
American Fork, Utah

Copyright © 2004 by Joni Hilton
All rights reserved. No part of this book may be reproduced in any format or in any medium without
the written permission of the publisher, Covenant Communications, Inc., P.O. Box 416, American
Fork, UT 84003. The views expressed herein are the responsibility of the author and do not necessarily
represent the position of Covenant Communications, Inc.

Printed in Canada
First Printing: August 2004

10 09 08 07 06 05 04   10 9 8 7 6 5 4 3 2 1

ISBN 1-59156-545-6

To Bob, Richie, Brandon, Cassidy, and Nicole—
the answers to so many of my prayers

TABLE OF CONTENTS

CHAPTER ONE

THE PURPOSE OF PRAYER

You can't pray a lie—I found that out.
—MARK TWAIN

Prayer is an ingenious gift from a Father who misses His children. He gave us this amazing tool in hopes that we would "call home" frequently and not lose touch. But it is more than just a way to stay in contact—it is a way to unlock the very powers of heaven, the key to a treasure box. Prayer can actually precipitate miracles. It can work mighty wonders in individual people and in the world at large. Because it is so very magical, many people dismiss it as exactly that: Magic. Pretend stuff. Something that can't possibly be real or truly work.

How wrong they are. Muttering familiar phrases to please a congregation probably doesn't work, that is true. But heartfelt, genuine pleading—in honest, sincere words of your own—can literally penetrate the veil and reach Heavenly Father Himself.

Most people, unless taught in a prayerful home, have no idea how to begin to speak with God. Millions of families across the world sit down to dinner, or rise in the morning, or go to bed at night and never even consider it. Some, fed up with the litany of chants and memorized prayers of their religion, conclude that these rituals have no practical application in their lives and abandon praying entirely. Intellectuals who scoff at religion imply that prayer has no real effect, that it is a holdover from less enlightened times. The media rarely mention prayer, and if it is acknowledged at all, it is only as a self-comforting concept. A few folks grow up afraid of a vengeful God, whose swift sword will punish sinners who dare approach Him. Some followers of charismatic preachers leave the praying to the experts and see it as a performance to be admired more than an actual connection with Deity. Praying has become a lost art.

Missionaries sometimes find that people aren't even clear about whom they're praying to—is He a mist, a blend of the Father and the Son, an everywhere-present something? How do you address someone whose form and shape you aren't even sure of? No wonder so many people are hesitant to pray.

As members of The Church of Jesus Christ of Latter-day Saints, we're taught that we are praying to an actual person, albeit a glorified one. He is the literal Father of our spirits. He created man in His own image. Thus, He looks like us. When we visualize a real personage, instead of some ambiguous force, we become more aware that our listener truly hears and loves us, and our prayers immediately become more intimate.

We know that God is not fearsome and tyrannical, as some believe Him to be. We know that the phrase "fear God" in the scriptures means to respect Him and give Him reverence, not to tremble because He is scary. We know that even the lowliest among us is still worthy to pray. We are not sinners who have lost that right—we are sinners who need that help! Even if we need correction or chastisement, it is not a mean-spirited God we approach, but a loving one who wants to guide us back onto the right path.

And we know that God and Christ are separate individuals; the notion of a combined trinity was created by committee in the fourth century in an effort to please everybody. No wonder it leaves such confusion even among those who want to believe what is right and true.

Many of us learned how to pray in our families or in Primary. Older converts are shown how to pray by the missionaries. But even among Church members, there is sometimes nervousness about praying in public, or concern that our private prayers are not as effective as they might be. Most of us would admit that too many of our prayers leave us feeling we missed the mark, as if we said the words but didn't have the "boosting power" to reach heaven.

That's what I want to change. Whether you've been praying all your life or you're just a beginner, my hope is that after reading this book your prayers will change. There will be a force and a power you can activate that will open a well of peace and happiness you never glimpsed before. You will develop a deeper relationship with God. You will have that "boosting power."

The first step is to understand the purpose of prayer. In a sentence, I can tell you this: Prayer is to bring your heart into line with God's. It is not a rote reciting; it is not giving God a "Dear Santa" wish list; it is not begging for things to be different than they are.

The real purpose of prayer is to refine your desires to match God's and to be of ultimate service to Him. It is to help you see things from an eternal perspective, so that you will ask for help in developing the strengths you need to meet your tasks. It is finding out what God wants for you, not telling God what you want for yourself.

Many of us learn to pray by following a basic list of the four main parts of prayer:

1. The opening: "Dear Father in Heaven,"
2. Thanking,
3. Asking,
4. The closing: "In the name of Jesus Christ, amen."

But this is just a rudimentary outline—truly a rough sketch of a prayer; it hardly begins to describe what praying can be like.

It is simply a guideline for learning how to pray and staying on track. It also reminds us that we always pray to God in the Son's name. Christ is our intermediary, our advocate with the Father. It is *through* Him that we pray to God the Father.

But prayer can be so much more than ticking off the list of blessings we're grateful for and additional ones we'd like. Prayer can teach us about God, our place in this world, the joys we've been overlooking, the exciting plans God has for us, and even what heaven will be like. It can cleanse our souls and change us into people of astounding strength to overcome weaknesses. It can save us from selfishness and sin, improve our health, and reach the hearts of others miles away. It can help us through the grieving process when we've suffered a loss. It can chase away loneliness. It can teach us things beyond our wildest dreams. It can, and has, changed the course of history.

Earnest prayer is never far from your thoughts. Real desire to know God's will doesn't just end when you say amen. Prayerful desires play upon your waking thoughts all day and continually pull you to a higher plane. Prayer is not the punctuation in an otherwise run-on sentence of a day. Prayer is the subject, the main focus—and daily life is the phrasing around it.

God has commanded us to pray, and He has done so since the beginning. When Adam offered sacrifices, an angel appeared and asked him why. Adam confessed that he didn't know why; he was simply obeying God's command. The angel then explained to him that this was in similitude of the sacrifice of Christ. "Wherefore, thou shalt do all that thou doest in the name of the Son, and thou shalt repent and call upon God in the name of the Son forever-more" (Moses 5:8).

Centuries later, Christ taught "that men ought always to pray, and not to faint" (Luke 18:1), and then on the American continent He instructed the Nephites to "pray always" as a protection from Satan, to pray in their families, and to pray in His name (see 3 Ne. 18:15–21).

Earlier in Nephite history, we find Nephi explaining Christ's doctrine to his brethren. He said, "If ye would hearken unto the Spirit which teacheth a man to pray ye would know that ye must pray; for the evil spirit teacheth not a man to pray, but teacheth him that he must not pray. But behold, I say unto you that ye must pray always, and not faint" (2 Ne. 32:8–9).

Alma, when passing on the mantle of leadership to his son, Helaman, advised him to "cry unto God for all thy support; yea, let all thy doings be unto the Lord, and whithersoever thou goest let it be in the Lord; yea, let all thy thoughts be directed unto the Lord; yea, let the affections of thy heart be placed upon the Lord forever. Counsel with the Lord in all thy doings, and he will direct thee for good; yea, when thou liest down at night lie down unto the Lord, that he may watch over you in your sleep; and when thou risest in the morning let thy heart be full of thanks unto God; and if ye do these things, ye shall be lifted up at the last day" (Alma 37:36–37).

What excellent advice, and it comes with the most glorious blessing possible—to be lifted up at the last day! How foolish we are if we disobey any commandment of God, but particularly one that can bring such improvement and joy into our lives. Being commanded to pray is like being commanded to breathe or to eat—it sustains our very souls, and if we forget to do it, we will wither spiritually, just as forgetting to eat will make us wither physically.

Prayer is a necessity. In modern times, Joseph Smith was told by the Lord to "continue in calling upon God in my name" (D&C 24:5). We cannot hope to accomplish even our noblest goals without enlisting God's help. Just as the ancient armies of Israel found that their reliance upon God determined their victory or their defeat, so will our success depend upon how truly we ask for God's hand in our lives. It is the only way to move forward with real faith and confidence. Our Founding Fathers pleaded for the Lord's help and inspiration in every meeting they held and every document they wrote. They would not even have considered doing otherwise and expect to triumph.

Remember when you pray that you are speaking to someone who knows all about you. He knows exactly what you need, already. But He wants *you* to know it. You are not teaching Him anything; you are teaching yourself.

He loves you and wants you to see that love in your life. Can you see the evidence of His love? Like any parent, He wants to hear you say you love Him too. Have you ever tried praying a prayer that simply expresses your love to Him, over and over? Try it, and see if tears do not fill your eyes as you realize you are speaking to the Author of love. Perhaps you will feel in your heart that no matter how much love you feel for your Father in Heaven, His love for you will always be greater. This is a humbling prayer that sweetens your life in a way nothing else can.

Prayer coaxes us to grow, yet keeps us childlike. It reminds us that the Master is the best one to steer our ship, not a mortal who can't see the whole picture yet, let alone the waterfall around the bend. Prayer helps us forgive others and find release from the bondage of grudge holding. Prayer teaches us to focus upon others, not just ourselves. Prayer reminds us that we have a loving Father in Heaven who is aware of us at every moment. Prayer teaches us that He wants to make miracles out of us. That may seem like a pretty tall order, but if it is to happen, prayer is our very best shot.

CHAPTER TWO·

THE LORD'S PRAYER

Our Father which art in heaven, Hallowed be thy name. Thy kingdom come. Thy will be done in earth, as it is in heaven. Give us this day our daily bread. And forgive us our debts, as we forgive our debtors. And lead us not into temptation, but deliver us from evil: For thine is the kingdom, and the power, and the glory, for ever. Amen.
—MATTHEW 6:9–13

Here, in just a few short lines, Jesus gives us the perfect pattern for prayer. It is everything a prayer should be—humble, sincere, appropriate, concise. It is a prayer which has been memorized by millions and repeated through the centuries, never outdated and never worn. Does it still apply to us today?

Absolutely.

Let's examine this sacred prayer line by line. Christ begins with a proper, respectful introduction, "Our Father which art in heaven," followed by immediate praise: "Hallowed be thy name." So much is implied in that phrase—an acknowledgment of God's supreme power, joy in His ultimate glory, how reverently we feel the brush of His name upon our lips, how much we love and adore Him. Hallowed means holy, sacred, divine, precious, and beloved. Christ is telling His Father of His great love and devotion for Him. What an ideal example for us to follow! When we pray, let us first revere God and let Him know of our gratitude and love for Him.

Next, Christ says, "Thy kingdom come." This means He is praying that God's kingdom will come, that His purposes will be fulfilled (including Christ's Atonement for us), and that God's whole plan of salvation will go as planned. Notice in the Book of Mormon version of the Lord's Prayer that this sentence is omitted (see 3 Ne. 13:9–13). This is because at the time Christ visited the Americas, He had already established His church, and God's kingdom *had* come.

"Thy will be done in earth, as it is in heaven." Christ continues His pledge to obey God's plan, and now He includes the Second Coming, when He shall reign personally upon the earth, all wickedness will end, and the earth shall be renewed.

When we speak this way, we submit to the will of the Father and express our desire to help build His kingdom and to make earth, ultimately, like heaven.

"Give us this day our daily bread." This phrase is also absent from the Book of Mormon version, because the Nephites were instructed to be grateful for what they already had. Today if we ask for "our daily bread," we are simply asking that God provide sustenance for us and allow us nourishment so that we can live another day to do whatever He asks of us. Around the world, this is no slight favor; hunger is common, and enough food to sustain life is a blessing indeed.

Next, Christ teaches us to beg forgiveness of the Father, to plead for mercy (none of us wants justice!). Following Christ's example, we promise to forgive one another, to extend love even to our enemies, to give all men the benefit of the doubt without designing our own punishment for them. "Forgive us our debts" also implies that God has given us more than we can pay for—and certainly this is true. The scales will never balance, even if we work all our lives to reimburse God for His goodness to us (see Mosiah 2:19–21). Thus, we ask Him not to require full payment, but to forgive us the difference, as we try our best. Likewise, we will not be harsh taskmasters with our fellow men, but loving and quick to overlook their shortcomings. Later, Christ talks of forgiving men their "trespasses" and tells us Heavenly Father will forgive ours in the same manner as we demonstrate forgiveness.

Next, Christ implores God for His hand to protect us from the adversary. Satan is dead serious in his battle to destroy our souls, and we must pray for God's help to defeat him. "Lead us not into temptation" doesn't mean that God would actually direct us into the devil's grasp. It simply means keep us from going there. Help us to recognize and avoid sin. Make us smart—too smart for the devil to ensnare. Keep us serious in our determination not to be fooled. Make us wise enough to avoid those places where temptation lurks.

It also acknowledges human frailty and how easily we can be thrown into doubt, swayed by our appetites, and seduced by power or acclaim. We want protection from those perils and deliverance when we stumble.

Christ closes with, "For thine is the kingdom, and the power, and the glory, for ever." How truly Christ understands the greatness of God and His endless blessings upon us! It's impossible to overstate God's glory. Twice now in one prayer, Christ has shown us the importance of acknowledging it. Our prayers should come from a grateful heart and should include worship and reverence for the Father. As we tell him that it is His kingdom, we also remind ourselves.

Bruce R. McConkie tells us that the Lord's Prayer is not designed for verbatim repetition in our prayers, and it doesn't conclude in the name of Jesus Christ as we are taught today, but it nevertheless illustrates the humble attitude with which we should approach our Maker (see *Mormon Doctrine*, 586–87).

It is important that we remember something most people don't think about in regard to prayer. Prayer isn't just a way to reach God. It's supposed to reach *you,* also, and remind you of your commitments. If you listen to your own words, prayer can help purify your soul, because you will come across the unmistakable fact of God's mercy and greatness. When we pray, we realize who's really in charge and whose plan will ultimately triumph. Our own petty concerns look out of place in this grand picture, don't they? As we acknowledge the importance of God's kingdom, our worldly concerns are seen in their true perspective, and we realize how unimportant some of them are.

Remember this: Praying not only reaches God but can teach you about the things that matter most. If we follow Christ's example, prayer should make God's priorities our priorities.

CHAPTER THREE

ELIMINATING TRITE LANGUAGE

Words without thoughts never to heaven go.
—WILLIAM SHAKESPEARE

Every culture has its sayings, its own language of the insiders, and members of The Church of Jesus Christ of Latter-day Saints are no different. Over the years, as we hear prayers in church and blessings on the food, certain phrases become quite familiar: *All our many blessings. Nourish and strengthen our bodies and do us the good we need. That everyone will go home safely and find all well there. The poor and the needy. Missionaries wherever they may be. That we may take these messages into our daily lives. Those who couldn't come this time, that they may come next time. And all other blessings we stand in need of.*

Now, first let me say that every one of these items is a good thing to pray for. The problem arises when we slip into verbal ruts so well-worn that they no longer require our attention. The clichés roll off our tongues without imparting any meaning. Christ said, "Use not vain repetitions, as the heathen do" (Matt. 6:7; see also 3 Ne. 13:7).

What's more, we come to expect these standard phrases and feel we are saying a "weird" prayer if we depart from them! If our prayers are laden with "Mormonisms" and little else, these sayings have become crutches and we a crippled people. Being able to string together a bunch of comfortable lines is not the same as praying from your heart, and, indeed, it will disable you from doing so.

When we are so preoccupied with thinking how our prayer is being received by the congregation, we have misdirected our very message. We're praying just to be perceived as someone who prays well, which Christ cautioned us never to do. He condemned the hypocrites who pray "that they may be seen of men" (Matt. 6:5; see also 3 Ne. 13:5).

We cannot serve both God and man, and we must choose one when we say a public prayer. Our prayers should come straight from our hearts in humility and love, whether smoothly worded or not. Prayers do not reach God's ears based upon sophisticated vocabulary or clever idioms. Praying is not performing! When we stop to worry how we're sounding, we lose our connection to the One we most want to reach.

There are several things we can do to eliminate trite language and improve the sincerity of our prayers. The first is to disregard the approval of others and to focus upon Heavenly Father instead. If others judge or criticize your prayer, the fault is theirs (although I cannot imagine this happening except in our own worried minds).

I once was asked to give a prayer for a large gathering of Relief Society sisters, and I was so thrilled about the day's events that I forgot to ask a blessing upon the meal that was to be served. Someone tapped me on the shoulder and asked me to say another prayer, and this time to include the food. Did this cause me great anguish and embarrassment? Not at all. I knew that Heavenly Father was probably smiling to Himself about how excited I get and how I tend to forget things, and I knew He understood me perfectly. I offered a second prayer, my spirits still soaring at the privilege it was to speak on behalf of so many of his daughters. The day went just fine. Stop worrying about what others are thinking or what you may have left out, and just speak with your Heavenly Father.

Second, the language of prayer improves when we concentrate on whom we're addressing. We are talking to our Father in Heaven.

Do you think He can't tell when we start mumbling cultural jargon? How would we feel if every time a friend spoke to us he said the exact same thing, the exact same way? "Hi John how's it goin' I'm fine give my regards to the family now we need to get together soon." We wouldn't feel very important to him, and we might even wonder about his mental state!

I have caught myself praying standard expressions when my mind drifts or my concentration falters. And I am always greatly embarrassed. I apologize to my Father, and I search my heart for words I really mean.

I find I concentrate better when I visualize Heavenly Father there with me, listening to my prayer. How would you speak if He were sitting beside you? You are not shouting through a megaphone that echoes through the galaxies, you know. This is intimate. This is close. He can hear your very thoughts. Keeping that in mind helps prevent drifting into clichés.

This does not mean that anything goes and that we can address Deity with the slang or casualness we might use when joking with a friend. We are to speak differently when addressing God. This helps us show the respect and honor due our God. We substitute the more formal "thee," "thou," "thy," and "thine" for "you," "your," and "yours." We also use "wilt," "shouldst," "canst," and the like. A more polite, reverent style of speech sets our prayers apart from our daily conversations and brings humility and tenderness into our supplications. When we adapt the proper language of prayer, we feel more comfortable addressing God Himself. And we find that our prayers that do not conform with this level of respect sound too familiar, almost impolite.

The third step in making our prayers more sincere is to think of alternative ways to say the things we're so accustomed to hearing. After all, we do want to pray for our food to be blessed and for people to go home safely. We just need to break out of the rote molds that have lost their meaning. Before you pray, think about the things you want to say and come up with a fresh way to say it. Try those phrases instead of falling back upon the old standbys.

Is there ever a time when prayers should be said with exact wording? Of course. Sacrament prayers and baptismal prayers are two examples, along with other ordinance prayers. But these commit us to solemn covenants and thus were given in exact wording by the Lord. Otherwise, we are not to use memorized prayers such as, "Now I lay me down to sleep."

Last, we need to eliminate the triteness of our closings.

Yes, we should close in the name of our Savior, and there is nothing wrong with saying, "We ask these things humbly in the name of Thy Son, Jesus Christ, amen." The only caution here has to do with speed. When we are closing a prayer in the name of our Redeemer, we need to slow down and think about what we are actually saying. To rush through and jumble it into "namaJesusChristamen" turns a beautiful phrase into another cliché. It's demeaning, it's disrespectful, and it breaks the reverence a prayer should have.

Listeners need to be able to echo your "amen" to affirm that they agree with your prayer and have been praying it right along with you. If all they heard at the end was a blur of syllables, it's harder to murmur a heartfelt amen.

Each of these steps will help make the language of your prayers more heartfelt. However, we must be careful not to rigidly apply these suggestions when we listen to others pray. This is, after all, a church of converts from all over the world. We want them to feel welcome praying in our meetings and not to worry that they don't have all the conventional platitudes memorized as they learn to pray. We may even find ourselves learning from their prayers. I always find new members' prayers refreshing in the same way children's prayers are: they are invariably from the heart, and you can almost feel a rush of wind as their prayers seem to ascend faster.

You can do this. It isn't hard to break the habit of trite language. You simply need to decide that you're someone who doesn't pray that way. I understand that a successful technique for breaking the habit of smoking is to define yourself as a nonsmoker. So it is with our prayers; we must define ourselves as people who pray sincerely. We know that using routine verbiage keeps our prayers from reaching their mark, from uplifting others, and from giving us a sense of real communion with our Maker. Once we decide we've left that world behind, we will have made strides in self-mastery the same way a smoker does who quits for good. We'll finally be praying our own prayers.

CHAPTER FOUR

THE PRAYER THAT WILL CHANGE YOUR LIFE

Two kinds of gratitude: the sudden kind
We feel for what we take, the larger kind
We feel for what we give.
—E. A. ROBINSON

Have you ever tried praying a prayer of only thanks? If you grew up as I did, thinking you always had to tack on a wish list, it's an interesting experience. I still remember my first attempt.

I was kneeling at my bed, listing all the usual things I was grateful for. I took a breath to begin my requests and then remembered that I was to leave it at that—just thanks and no asking for stuff. It felt very short and oddly incomplete! I was so used to winding up with a focus on my personal desires and needs that to skip Step Three felt distinctly abnormal. Shame on me. What must Heavenly Father have been thinking all these years—*When is she going to get it?* I paused and tried to think of some more things I was thankful for, so my prayer wouldn't look so puny.

And suddenly I broke through. I could see an infinite array of things to be thankful for beyond my usual list. It even included things I didn't know I was grateful for—some obstacles and trials I'd recently had, which I had not realized had actually benefited me. This was it—this was being thankful in all things, as we are told to do in Doctrine and Covenants 98:1. I suddenly realized that every experience, if we learn from it, can be for our good. The

Lord tells us that "all things wherewith you have been afflicted shall work together for your good, and to my name's glory" (D&C 98:3). So events are not only things we can learn from, but things which show the glory of God. How wrong we are to try to pray away those things which testify of our Father in Heaven!

This means our gratitude must never waver, even when life's storms seem insurmountable. Gratitude forms the basis of our worship. Knowing we are children of God, and being eternally thankful for it, we can survive every test that comes our way. The key: *Look for the lesson in it.*

Remember when Christ healed ten lepers but only one returned to thank him? (see Luke 17:12–19). Gratitude is a rare commodity among us mortals. And we are no better than the nine ungrateful lepers when we pray for something (even safety on a trip) and then forget to pray our thanks when the petition is granted.

Throughout holy writ, we are cautioned against ingratitude. It is a sin of considerable weight and not to be taken lightly: "And in nothing doth man offend God, or against none is his wrath kindled, save those who confess not his hand in all things, and obey not his commandments" (D&C 59:21). On the flip side, "He who receiveth all things with thankfulness shall be made glorious; and the things of this earth shall be added unto him, even an hundred fold, yea, more" (D&C 78:19).

So how can you show that you appreciate God's blessings? You can share them with others. You can live worthy of them by keeping God's commandments and striving for purity in thoughts and actions. And you can pray your thanks unceasingly.

Imagine sending a child away to college, helping her immeasurably, and never hearing a word of thanks. Actually, that's probably an all-too-common experience! But in a way, it's also a common experience for our Father in Heaven, and that is a travesty.

Now imagine you do hear thanks from your child, but every time she thanks you, she asks for even more. Sound familiar? This is why prayers of *only thanks* are so vital. We do not have to constantly add requests when we communicate with God. Sometimes gratitude is simply enough.

Now let's look at the second kind of gratitude, the "larger kind we feel for what we give." It's sort of a "higher law" of gratitude. Yes, you can be thankful for all that you have—for your pile of worldly wealth and your comfortable surroundings—but it's still a gratitude based on yourself.

The second kind is based on what you're able to give others. If you have more than you need and can donate to charity, you have been entrusted with an extra stewardship—the disbursement of your excess. This kind of gratitude also includes the giving of our time, of our knowledge, and of our services.

Helping someone in need gives a sheen to your soul—your heart changes. You feel (and are) more vital, more important. Your "valuable player" status has grown, and you sense that you are working as a partner with God to bless others. Suddenly, life isn't about how much you can accumulate or what you "get" anymore. Selfishness has evaporated and left a purer person behind: someone who is focused on giving and is grateful to have the chance.

Have you ever done a Sub-for-Santa Christmas, where you gather gifts for a needy family and deliver them anonymously? Have you felt the energy and joy in the air as you've all climbed back into the car and sped away? It's exciting—almost like a liquid pouring into your soul and filling the spaces where self-centeredness used to be. It tingles, enlivens, and enlarges your spirit.

We feel grateful for the opportunity to do something for someone else. It's love in action, love the way the Savior taught it. This kind of giving makes us grateful in a completely different way than appreciation for "things." Our prayers change, as we humbly thank God for making use of us, for putting us in a situation where we could do something for Him.

It also makes our troubles look smaller and more manageable.

It puts mortal worries into perspective and gives us greater things to focus on than flat tires and bad hair days. We become preoccupied with eternal matters that bring real satisfaction: comforting a lonely widow, cheering up a sick child, easing the burdens of an overwhelmed mother, guiding a lost soul back into light. It's hard to worry about the color of the dinner-party napkins when you've been teaching literacy all day at the library or sharing your testimony of Christ with someone at work.

If you want to change your life dramatically—and instantly—try this experiment. Pray to Heavenly Father to guide you to someone to help. Then, everywhere you go, look for that person. You walk into the post office and see a grumpy person in line? Give him a hand with his packages. You go to the airport and see a frazzled mother trying to scoot along her luggage and calm a crying baby? Help her. (President Gordon B. Hinckley first told the story of President Spencer W. Kimball doing exactly this during the December 1983 First Presidency Christmas Devotional.) You see a short person reaching for something on the top shelf at the supermarket? Stop and get it for them.

Slow down. Deliberately make time for good deeds. If you know you'll only need an hour at the mall, give yourself an hour and twenty minutes—who knows how many people you'll see who need help once you start looking for them?

Is there someone struggling out there who has lost faith in humankind, who feels the world has turned cold and selfish? Can you restore someone's faith and create a ripple effect whose far-reaching effects you can't even calculate? Can you find a friend who needs the knowledge you have? Can you make a difference in the world today?

You can. And when you take this approach to the world around you, all your perceptions will change. Suddenly, it will be as if someone switched on the lights. Your days will be more fulfilling, your schedule less taxing, your family members more enjoyable, your health better, your coworkers happier, your obligations less burdensome, your prayers more meaningful. You will multiply your joy quotient. And your prayers will be filled to overflowing with gratitude.

CHAPTER FIVE

PRESENTING A PLAN IN PRAYER

Pray as if everything depended upon God,
and work as if everything depended upon you.
—ANONYMOUS

Many times we find our lives so beset with problems and confusion that we cry out for God's help—we pray for solutions or decisions that we can't fathom by ourselves. A task looks utterly impossible, a situation seems doomed to failure, we make mistakes that look irreparable, we are confronted with choices and can't choose one.

Most people share their dilemma with God, then wait for the answer to fall into their laps—a new employee who will work for free, a shift in the climate so we can have an outdoor wedding reception in January, a magic cure for alcoholism, an A on a test we didn't study for—crazy stuff.

And then, when those "genie wishes" don't happen, these are the people who say prayer doesn't work.

Prayer doesn't make problems magically evaporate. That isn't how it works.

When we are praying for a specific answer, for wisdom, for help with decisions, there's actually a formula that makes prayer work. We can actually know God's will, eliminate the guesswork, and discern the best decision. The Savior tells us exactly how to do this:

> Behold, you have not understood; you have supposed that
> I would give it unto you, when you took no thought save it
> was to ask me. But, behold, I say unto you, that you must
> study it out in your mind; then you must ask me if it be
> right, and if it is right I will cause that your bosom shall
> burn within you; therefore, you shall feel that it is right.
> But if it be not right you shall have no such feelings, but
> you shall have a stupor of thought that shall cause you to
> forget the thing which is wrong. (D&C 9:7–9)

The secret is to present a plan, not just a wad of hysteria for God to sort through. Remember, He already knows what's best—He wants you to learn it also. Begin by thinking through the situation carefully and formulating an approach. Use a paper and pencil, if necessary. Get respected opinions. Do your research. Think of every solution you can possibly imagine. If you're deciding between taking two jobs, consider that perhaps neither one is right. Or maybe they both are, part-time. Consider every option. After thoughtfully analyzing your dilemma, design a strategy.

Now take it to Father in Heaven, and see if your plan was right. How will you know? You'll feel it in your heart. If God approves of your conclusion, you'll feel great—it will be as if a warmth and a clarity is filling your mind, and you'll have a positive desire to enact your plan. There will be a distinct sense of peace and well-being. You won't mistake it for your own feelings because it will feel different—holier, warmer, clearer. When you do something utterly selfless for someone and you're suddenly caught off guard by a rush of joy, it's that same feeling.

If your plan is wrong, you'll experience confusion and cloudy thinking. You might even forget the plan in midprayer. You will not feel settled or comfortable, and your troubles will still loom as large as ever.

What do you do in these instances? You go back to the drawing board and work out a different solution. You bring Him the new idea and "listen" all over again. And you repeat this process until you get the right answer.

Sometimes we keep praying for our favorite choice. We know all along what plan God wants, but we're trying to talk Him into something that seems easier or more appealing to us. "Oh, *please* don't let us move away—I love living here and we have such good friends and the kids are happy in school . . ." This is just begging, and in your heart you know it. To really get a firm answer, you have to put aside your personal wants and wishes and truly seek to know God's will. He knows what's best for you in the long run. He knows where He needs you. He knows problems unseen to you, which can crop up if you don't follow His counsel. He has much better things in store for you, just as you do for your children when they whine to stay up late. He is your parent, and He can see the big picture.

To put our lives in His hands is a scary thought, especially if you're someone who wants to know all the ins and outs before you take a risk. But guess what's even scarier? Flying solo. Deciding not to listen and to submit to God's will is absolutely like jumping off a cliff. You have no guarantees whatsoever. The safest course of action is actually to put your trust in God and let Him lead. But, like all children, most of us are slow to learn this lesson. Remember: The leap of faith is always into God's arms.

The perfect model of this method is in the book of Ether, when the brother of Jared has been instructed to move his people, via submarine, to a new land—and it occurs to him that in airtight boats, they will have no light. He asks the Lord about this, and instead of instantly solving the problem, the Lord puts it back into the hands of the brother of Jared: "What will ye that I should do that ye may have light in your vessels?" (Ether 2:23).

The brother of Jared must now formulate a plan of his own—he must think of a way to light these boats, then take his idea to the Lord. So he goes to the top of a mountain where he can melt sixteen glassy stones from rock, and he asks, with unflinching faith, for the

Lord to touch them and make them shine. His faith is so great that not only does the Lord do this, but Christ allows the brother of Jared to see Him—a first at that point in his people's history.

We need to present our "stones" in a similar manner—and see if this is what the Lord wants us to do. Consider an example.

You want a raise. Your kids need braces, the house needs painting, and you need a new washer and dryer. You haven't had a raise in a long time, but you've steadily helped the company grow. You decide you'll tell your boss of your needs and see if you get the raise. You kneel down and present the plan to God.

You don't feel steady or secure though. Something is amiss. You sense you won't get the desired results with the plan you've presented. The anxiety is still there.

So you meditate and think harder about the situation. You put yourself in your boss's place. What would he want to hear? What would convince him that you're worth more than he's currently paying you?

Now you have another approach. This time you pray, "I'm planning to show my boss the increased profits of the last six months, along with the extra training I got on my own time. I'll show how much better my department is running, and I'll include my last four job reviews, with the favorable comments from my supervisor. I won't mention my expenses—only my performance, my value to the company."

Suddenly it feels right. You feel infused with enthusiasm to carry out this second plan. Confident and filled with peace, you know you have an answer to your prayer.

And sure enough, your boss is a bottom-line man who wants to see dollar-and-cent profits. He doesn't respond to emotional pleas or stories about personal crises—he figures people should make a budget and live within their means if they've got bills. He rewards performance, period. You get the raise.

You found the right stones.

Let's look at another example.

Your son has been caught cheating on a test. He's been thrown off the basketball team and suspended from high school for a week. The record of his cheating will stay in his file and affect college applications. He spends all his time in his bedroom and lashes out angrily whenever anyone tries to talk to him. You have no idea what to do. You agonize for his future, you're angry at him for making such a stupid choice, you're humiliated because everyone knows, you're ashamed that you didn't raise a more honest boy, you're appalled that he doesn't seem more humble about it all, you're mad at your neighbor for her condescending attitude—the list goes on and on.

You want to pray for guidance, but your mind is a jumble of emotions. You think it over and decide to take the reins, lead out with strength and standards, and give that boy a clear message that cheating will not be tolerated in this family. He'll be grounded for a month and won't be able to drive the family car for three months. There'll be no back talk and no more of this sullen pouting. No sir, it's time to realize that he's hurt the team, his family, and everybody else.

You kneel down with this detailed plan in mind and present it to your Father. But it just hangs there. Like wet laundry. You don't feel soothed or calmed. In fact, you feel worked up and angry.

You turn to the scriptures to try to get the Spirit back so you can pray. After some concentration and meditation, you reconsider your plan. Maybe your measures need to be harsher. After all, you never did give your son a proper lecture when it first happened. You pray about being even more severe.

But now you feel enveloped in darkness. You are definitely going in the wrong direction. You acknowledge your failure to come up with the right idea, and you plead and cry to God for help. How can you resolve this horrible situation?

Suddenly it comes into your mind how God has dealt with you during your darkest hours. You remember how He allowed you to suffer consequences those many years ago, but how He was the one loving soul you could turn to, the only One! He was your strength, the hand cupped gently under you as you fell, He who caught you just in time. That's it!

You begin a new prayer with a new plan. This time your plan is much simpler. You will extend unconditional love to your son. You will be there for him to let him know that life is not over and that you still believe in him. He is already suffering enough, and he knows acutely how disappointed his friends and family are. Suddenly, you realize that his anger is anger at himself for making such an awful mistake and bringing so much heartache to those he cares about. You rise to your feet with a renewed sense of peace. The problem has not lifted, but your plan of action is blessed by God; He will endorse this one. By loving your son through his ordeal, you will cement bonds of love he will never forget. There will still be suffering and learning for your son, but he will also learn about mercy and forgiveness. Years from now, he will become a better husband and father for it.

You found the right stones.

One last example.

You have a wonderful chance to join your husband on a week-long business trip in Hawaii. You proceed to make arrangements for your children, farming them out to various relatives and friends, setting up someone to water the plants, and deciding which sundresses to take along. It hardly seems like something to pray about, other than giving thanks for a great opportunity.

Even the practical arrangements have fallen perfectly into place.

Still, you kneel to pray one afternoon, and you present your plan.

Suddenly you feel a sense of concern, a gnawing similar to those times when you wonder if you've left the oven on. The feeling grows—something is not right. You dismiss it as fatigue. After all, it's exhausting to tie up so many loose ends before a vacation. You continue your day, and when your best friend tells you to stop worrying, that you've earned a second honeymoon, you agree. That night, when you kneel to pray, you feel a distinct sense of foreboding. You run through the arrangements in your mind—you'll cancel the paper and hold the mail—what else could it be? There's a heaviness in your chest and a prompting to change your plans.

But you don't want to change your plans! You want to go to Hawaii! Why would anyone pray anything else? You climb into bed, but you cannot sleep.

Finally, you get down on your knees again, and this time you submit your heart to Heavenly Father. This time you tell Him that you are canceling your vacation and staying home while your husband goes on the trip without you. You're sure this can't be right, and you wait to feel even more unsettled than ever.

But instead, you feel light, buoyed up, and almost brimming with tears of joy and relief. This makes no sense at all. Logically, there is every reason to go on the trip. But here you are, praying about staying home, and feeling *right,* straight down to your toes. You have no idea why God is keeping you from going to Hawaii.

In the morning, you share your revelation, and your husband prays with you. He, too, gets the same odd inspiration that there is some reason for you to stay home. You are tempted to ignore this answer as you have never been tempted before! But you cancel the babysitters and tell your husband to have a wonderful time. As you wave good-bye to him at the airport, you smile and shrug. "I sure hope God knows what He's doing," you think silently.

Two nights later you awaken suddenly with an urge to check on your youngest child. You find her soaking wet, thrashing in the midst of a grand mal seizure, and you call an ambulance. You spend the next two days in the hospital and learn that your daughter has epilepsy and that, had you not acted so quickly, she would have had brain damage. You fall to your knees in prayer, thankful to a loving Heavenly Father who prompted you to stay home, and you wonder how you could ever have forgiven yourself had you ignored His warning.

You found the right stones.

Sometimes we don't want to present the unpleasant choice, because we're afraid God will say, "Yes, that's the one." We want the other person to say he's sorry—not for us to apologize. We want someone else to accept the calling of nursery leader, not follow a prompting to *volunteer* for it, for heaven's sake. We want to buy the dream house, not settle for one that fits more snugly within our budget. We want to choose our buddies to work with on the ward committee, not that irksome member who keeps coming to mind when we pray about it. We want to keep our cloak of pride wrapped tightly about our shoulders, and when God tugs to pull it away, sometimes we yank back, resisting the ultimate happiness He knows is in our best interest. It's not easy to let go of our personal desires and see what God wants.

It takes courage to pray this way, to really put our hearts on the line and let God choose. But I've never met anyone who regretted it. Sometimes He asks us to do tough things, to be greater than we think we are. But He also stays right beside us and helps us do it. Afterward, when we see that He was right, we invariably marvel and think, "Of course! God knew all along," as if we are amazed that our Maker should be so smart.

What a patient parent He is. How slow to learn are so many of His children! And yet he loves us and waits, infinitely kind and always willing to tell us when our choices are correct.

We just have to find the right stones.

CHAPTER SIX

THE POWER OF PRAYER

More things are wrought by prayer
Than this world dreams of.
—ALFRED TENNYSON

The greatest events in history have all begun with prayer. Think about it. From the beginning of time when Adam built an altar, prayer has precipitated the miraculous. Abraham's petition to the Lord resulted in a posterity greater than the sands of the sea. Moses prayed for help leading the children of Israel out of Egypt. David prayed for God's help in slaying Goliath. Armies defending freedom have prevailed against all odds by praying. Columbus was led to the Americas in response to his prayers. Righteous nations have been founded by prayerful pilgrims. Even the Restoration of the gospel of Jesus Christ came in response to a prayer. And greatest of all, the Atonement of Christ was accomplished through prayer.

Is there a more powerful force in the universe? When we pray, if we are righteous and obedient, we form a bond with God—we unite with him in a common purpose and make a working agreement. We have offered to learn His will and then do it, and God has offered to grant us the strength to accomplish the seemingly impossible. He will not go back on His word. "I, the Lord, am bound when ye do what I say; but when ye do not what I say, ye have no promise" (D&C 82:10). This means that if we are living to the best of our abilities, we can call upon the forces of heaven to work righteousness according to God's will.

One of the best ways to see the power of prayer in action is to pray for our enemies. This counsel makes most of us squirm, even though we all know how pointedly Christ taught it. But what most of us don't realize is that when you can really bring yourself to pray for blessings upon those that hate you, you get a double answer. You've asked for peace and joy for people who really need it, but the most miraculous result is what happens to you—you grow spiritually by leaps and bounds. You free yourself from bitterness and resentment, and you experience inner calm and joy as never before. God can choose whether He wants to bless your enemies or not, but the very act of praying for them blesses *you*. It illustrates the immense power of prayer, right in your heart.

One of the most dramatic events in the Book of Mormon is recorded in Alma 36—and the events related are in direct response to fervent prayer. Alma the Younger, who has rebelled against his father and the Church, is visited by an angel whose appearance causes Alma to fall to the ground paralyzed, unable to move or speak for three days. When young Alma finally regains his strength, he has become "born of God" (v. 26) and makes a complete turnaround. He becomes one of the greatest leaders in all of recorded history, a man of immense courage and conviction. But what brought about this miraculous event? The prayers of Alma's parents. I'm sure there was more than one anguished prayer uttered in his behalf (and in behalf of his friends, who also made complete turnarounds). Parents who know the sorrow of wayward children offer heartfelt prayers like almost no one else's.

We do not know how long it took for the timing to be right and for Alma to be receptive to God's message. But we can be sure his parents asked in faith, "nothing wavering," as we're told to do in James 1:6. And they did not give up, but kept believing until God chose the perfect moment to reach their son.

As members of The Church of Jesus Christ of Latter-day Saints, we've often heard the phrase "Exercise faith." But what does that mean? Have faith in Jesus Christ, that He is our Redeemer? Have faith that things will work out? Have faith that God hears us?

Exercising faith means all that and more. It means *really believing*. It means you have prayed, and you are absolutely certain God is watching over you and will help you if it is His will. Now you must stop fretting. Continuing to doubt and worry demonstrates a *lack* of faith. Catholic Bishop Fulton J. Sheen said, "All worry is a form of atheism, because it's a want of trust in God" (*Inspirational Quotations,* 478). To enact the power of miracles, you must stop pacing and wringing your hands. Take a deep breath, know that God is steering the ship, and simply believe.

There is tremendous peace in exercising pure faith. And there is tremendous power as well, particularly if we are praying for a miracle. Faith is the foundation for miracles, just as gravity is the foundation of the laws of physics. God works within laws, and faith is one of them. In Ether 12:12 we read, "For if there be no faith among the children of men God can do no miracle among them," and in Mosiah 8:18 we are told that "God has provided a means that man, through faith, might work mighty miracles."

Have you ever needed a real miracle? I can recall several times in my life when I've had to call upon God for intervention beyond mortal power. Some of these times have dealt with health emergencies, getting messages through to others, reaching lost souls, and even surviving desperate dangers.

In each case when I've needed a miracle, I've noticed that asking for the situation to disappear is the wrong approach. Closing your eyes during a horror movie doesn't really make the monsters go away, either. That's just like trying to run away from what frightens us.

No, God does not want us to run away. He wants us to summon our faith and turn to Him. He will show us how to conquer adversity and become a better people. That can't happen if we refuse to acknowledge a crisis or if we stick our heads in the sand until the problem goes away (usually it only gets worse).

Sometimes we need to pray for nearly superhuman powers to endure suffering or pain. Many situations will not change in our lifetime, and we must find a way to cope and work with the existing scenario—early widowhood, divorce, memories of child-hood abuse, unwed motherhood, a handicapped child, physical limitations, and so on. In these instances, we must stop praying to be someone else or someplace else and face reality.

There are lessons in our trials that will refine us and that God expects us to learn. He wants our "soul muscles" to strengthen. We're more valuable to Him that way, and more valuable to others and ourselves. As the saying goes, God doesn't help us out of our problems; He helps us through them. When you think of being faithful, think of faith-*full*.

Sometimes we need to pray for patience, tolerance, forgiveness, and the other "quiet virtues" that help us accept choices made by others. We develop many of these traits as we wait for our prayers to be answered. Often we discover that it is God waiting for us, not the other way around. When we finally develop the skill and the humility we are supposed to—or have finally given up our sins or doubts—*then* He answers our prayers.

He also waits for us to stop comparing our load of burdens with the next person's. Comparing outward trials and concluding that someone else has an easier life is one of the adversary's most powerful tools. If he can get us to pity ourselves and give in to discouragement, Satan has built a valuable foundation for heaping even more misery upon us, and he keeps us from praying effectively.

Before I reached the age of eight, every one of my grandparents had died. When I was twelve, my only sibling, an older sister, was killed. When I was in my twenties, my dad died. Many aunts, uncles, and cousins followed. Most of my friends had never experienced such losses, and there were times when I used to wonder if I was being given too much grief to handle. But the Lord knows the capabilities of each of us, and He had given me strength to survive these losses and to be of use to others experiencing the death of loved ones.

Through tragedy, He showed me what I was made of, taught me how to learn from heartache, and helped me see that through every setback He is there to pull me along. I cannot compare my troubles to others'; they have their own challenges to meet, tailored to address each of their weaknesses. Other people may not need the lessons I did, and I may not need the ones yet ahead for them. But as we pray about the difficulties we encounter in life, God will show us how to cope, how to survive, how to take one breath after another, and how to endure when all appears lost. He will send the Comforter, and we will again know peace.

To be sure, we learn humility. We learn how weak and helpless we are, how very much we depend upon God. Trials sharpen this perspective and remind us that without Him we are nothing, that humility is the key to unlocking the power of prayer. We learn firsthand that prayer only works when we're truly humble and submit our will to the Lord's.

Sometimes when we pray for what seems to be a small thing, we discover just how powerful prayer is. God surprises us by giving us an avalanche of blessings—much more than we had even requested. Isn't this like the best moments of parenting? You want so much to show your children that you love them, that you're there for them, that you want them to find joy. If they ask for your help in the right attitude, there's almost nothing you wouldn't do for them, right? I'm not talking about just giving them material goods, but giving them opportunities, privileges, trust, and gifts of the Spirit. God is the perfect parent and likewise wants to bless us even more than we hope.

There's a wonderful description of this in Matthew 7:11: "If ye then, being evil, know how to give good gifts unto your children, how much more shall your Father which is in heaven give good things to them that ask him?"

He *can't wait* for us to reach the level of humility and godly motivation so He can shower us with blessings, especially the blessing of the Holy Ghost. If we have brought our hearts in line with His, as I discussed in chapter 1, He is like the father of the prodigal son, ready to embrace us and arrange a feast. "I have heard thy prayer, I have seen thy tears: behold, I will heal thee" (2 Kgs. 20:5).

Know that the righteous desires you have, however small, matter to God, because they matter to you. Just as you care about your children's concerns, He cares about yours. The Maker of the Universe, the Creator of Mankind, the God of Moses and Abraham still hears your cries and loves you unspeakably. Elder Marvin J. Ashton said, "Nothing is too unimportant for God" (*Prayer,* 76). Do not be afraid to approach the Lord with matters you think are too trivial for one so great. You are a crowning glory to Him, a choice spirit who chose His plan and came to earth. He will never be too busy for you.

Have you ever had the experience of praying humbly for something small and then being completely astonished at an answer that completely exceeds your grandest hopes? On numerous occasions I have felt tears rushing to my eyes as I stared in wonder at what was clearly divine intervention—pointed answers to specific prayers that went so gloriously beyond my expectations that I literally gasped with joy and gratitude.

I asked my husband, Bob, if he would mind my sharing the story of a tough time we had early in our marriage. Bob had been baptized before our marriage, but he became overwhelmed with the spiritual expectations of being the priesthood leader in our home, and he told me he began to doubt his testimony.

My heart was broken, and all I can tell you is that Heavenly Father cupped His hands and caught the pieces. I cannot count the tears or the prayers of that time. I think both were constant. I really did pray all day long and most of each night. Even as I was driving, or cooking, or bathing my little ones, prayers ran through my head. I wanted a husband who was fully committed to the same things we had agreed upon before we married.

Four months ticked by as I fasted and prayed for Bob to remember his testimony. My bishop and several friends fasted with me. I made calls and wrote letters to several Church members, begging them to pray for him.

I pored over the scriptures for comfort and direction. One night I prayed to turn to the exact scripture that could help me and flipped the scriptures open to the pointed advice for Emma Smith in Doctrine and Covenants 25:5. At Relief Society that Sunday, the lesson seemed directed specifically toward me, emphasizing that we must preserve marriage and support our husbands. I finally realized that I must accept my situation and allow Bob his agency to choose for himself. My duty was to preserve the marriage and not make it contingent upon Church dedication. That was the answer to all my prayers. It was one of the hardest choices I've ever had to make. Bob could see what I was willing to do, and he offered me a promise: he would continue to pray and try to gain a testimony, for however long it took. He knew he had been selfish and scared and was determined to make it up to me.

General conference was coming up, and Bob agreed to attend it with me. I felt it was imperative that I get him to Salt Lake and let him somehow meet some leaders. Anybody would do—I had a picture in my mind of him shaking hands with some wonderful man whose personality, brilliance, and spirituality would touch Bob and motivate him to come back. I got the crazy idea to try to make an appointment with a General Authority but soon discovered that if you want to meet with a Church leader, general conference time is the busiest, and thus worst, time to try to wedge into someone's schedule.

We boarded the plane without any appointments, but I kept praying. He just *had* to meet someone. *Anyone.* I would not let go of that silent prayer. We watched all the sessions and attended one in person in the Tabernacle. When the members of the Twelve and First Presidency entered the room, I could feel the Spirit wash over me, and tears flooded my eyes. Again, in silent prayer, I pleaded with Heavenly Father to help Bob meet someone who could help him feel the way I did about these men.

The next day was Monday, and conference had ended. Our flight wasn't until that evening, so I suggested we drive through the canyons to see the fall colors. At one point, we found ourselves in Heber, and I wanted to show Bob the Homestead restaurant and resort, which I remembered visiting with my family. After walking around the grounds, we stopped by the lobby for a brochure. I glanced into the dining room and saw a woman who looked exactly like Flora Benson. And then my heart stopped: It *was* Sister Benson. I kept staring after she passed the doorway, and then, to my utter amazement, there was President Benson himself, walking right behind her with some of his relatives.

"It's President Benson!" I whispered, clutching Bob's arm.

"Well, go tell him hello," Bob said.

"I can't!" I whispered back. "I'm wearing track shoes." I felt entirely unpresentable in my casual attire.

And then, suddenly, he was walking toward us, reaching out to shake hands. My eyes filled with tears, and as they spilled down my cheeks, I blurted, "I love you. Thank you so much."

His grandson explained that their family tradition was always to have lunch at the Homestead the Monday after conference. President Benson looked into my face and said, "As my wife would say, may the Lord bless you and the devil miss you."

Bob chuckled, always one to appreciate a sense of humor, then reached out and shook his hand. Even under Bob's sunglasses, you could see the tears. He was electrified. Touching the hand of a prophet of God reawakened his testimony and, in an instant, had given me back my husband.

As the prophet walked off, I ran a few feet behind him, trying to put my feet in exactly the same spots that he had. I felt like a child again, stripped down to my real soul, simply wanting to bask in the glow of his light, to be like him, if only in my footsteps.

I turned to face Bob. He was dissolved with joy and with the witness in his heart that this was a prophet of God. I couldn't believe what had just happened. I had prayed for months, had finally listened, and then had prayed for "just anybody" to meet Bob and make a difference. The Lord had answered my prayer so far beyond my humblest hopes that I still can hardly believe the magnitude of His love in giving me so much more than I asked for. I will never believe that this was mere coincidence.

Today Bob is far beyond my wildest dreams. He is a spiritual giant, a former high councilor, a fantastic father (of four), and a frequent testimony-bearer. He's a bold missionary, a pillar of strength, and a faithful priesthood leader for our family. He loves the temple, and he loves the Lord. He spends nearly every free minute of his time serving neighbors and ward members, exactly as Christ wants us to. He'll jump up in the night and put on a tie to go and give someone a blessing, he'll help people move heavy boxes even though he has a bad back, and he's first to every activity to help set up chairs, welcome new members, or help in any way he can. The greatest compliment I ever saw someone give him was when the Young Women presented Bob with an apron that said "Chair Man" to acknowledge his dependability and service. That is exactly what I always wanted: a man who would be an active ward member, one who gets in and does the work.

I know many sisters wait a lot longer than four months for their husbands to come around. But I also know that Heavenly Father hears their prayers and will bless them for their faithfulness and for supporting their husbands without reservation. His timetable is different for each one of us, but I can truly testify that He hears and answers our prayers. Miracles are what He does. I know, because I'm married to one.

CHAPTER SEVEN

PRAYER IN THE FAMILY

*The man who will pray morning, noon and night and
humble himself before the Lord, and pray to the
Lord in his prosperity just as he would pray to
Him in his adversity . . . will never apostatize.*
—JOSEPH F. SMITH

Of all the examples you could give to your children, praying together as a family is probably the strongest. When children know that their family is united in a daily report to God, acknowledging His greatness, thanking Him for blessings, and praying for one another, they are blessed throughout their lives with faith, purpose, loyalty, and a solid base of security.

Children who pray with their parents realize adults aren't all-powerful and all-knowing. They see that grown-ups, too, take their burdens to God and ask for help. It establishes an important pattern of humility and living a Christ-centered life. They learn to seek God's will in their daily activities, to turn to the Lord when they have troubles, and to present a well-thought-out plan to their Maker.

Likewise, they see that prayer is not just an emergency kit for hard times, but a daily offering, even when life is rolling along smoothly. They learn that prayers can be just as sincere when life is good as when we find ourselves in dire circumstances. They learn to pray heartfelt gratitude.

They also learn to offer themselves to God as His servants. They gain an understanding of their relationship with Him and learn what He expects them to do.

The promise of blessings to those who pray as a family comes from above. The Savior commanded, "Pray in your families unto the Father, always in my name, that your wives and your children may be blessed" (3 Ne. 18:21).

Teaching children to pray should start at the very beginning of their lives. Holding an infant in your arms while prayer is offered is the first introduction. They are not too young; they can feel the Spirit and can understand more than they can communicate back. As they get old enough, children can learn to kneel with the family and to fold their arms as a sign of reverence. As soon as they can speak (or sooner, if they wish to try), children should be given the opportunity to pray. It is a privilege to speak in behalf of the family, and it should be portrayed as such, not simply as a turn to take.

Usually parents teach their children by saying a few words at a time and having the child repeat the words. This trains children in the proper language of prayer and the kinds of things we pray about. While such prayers are usually short and simple, we should take extra care to pray from the heart so we don't pass on pat phrases. As problems or blessings arise during the day, these are good times to kneel with children and teach them the importance of prayer. Young children will often experience losing a cherished belonging. Praying to find it and discovering that God is indeed there and will guide them to the item can be memorable and important moments in the development of a testimony. And they are humbling moments for adults as we remember that God loves us and cares about our smallest worries.

Children also discover in the home that when you least feel like praying is the time when you most need to. If parents do not teach this important lesson, who will?

In addition to learning how to pray a family prayer, a prayer in class at church, and a blessing on the food, children need to be taught to have their own personal, private prayers. These are the moments when they can pour out their hearts to God, confess weaknesses, and hear individual revelations.

Teaching our children to pray is more than just a good idea; it is a commandment. In 1831 the Lord told Joseph Smith that members "shall also teach their children to pray, and to walk uprightly before the Lord" (D&C 68:28). If we fail to train our children, we must answer for that omission.

Children who come from praying families never forget how to pray. Even if they experience a period of confusion or inactivity, they will remember how to connect with their Lord when they choose to. It's like learning to ride a bike; you just never forget.

Sometimes our children can feel when we are praying for them. Many missionaries have reported a distinct impression of times when their families were asking for God's protection for them. Those who are spiritually lost or sick have also felt the prayers of others in their behalf. If you establish traditions of praying for your children before a test in school or at other times when they need God's help, they will know that when test time comes, you are right there praying along with them. It's a way to connect with one another, as well as with our Heavenly Father.

Children should also be encouraged to pray for others outside the immediate family. When you pray with them, include your extended family, ward members with special needs, children and teachers at school, and people they read about across the world who are coping with tragedy and hardship. We are a united world family of God's children, and our kids need to grow up feeling love for all humanity and a desire to help.

They also need to learn that simply mumbling a prayer for those in need is not enough. Teach them to take a plan of action to Heavenly Father and see if He can use it. What if we donated blankets to the refugees? First aid supplies to the flood victims? Toys to the children at a shelter? What if we invited the grocer and his wife to dinner? What if we helped clean up at the campground for kids with special needs? Asking the Lord to help those with challenges doesn't mean, "We hope you find someone else to do this." It means, "We care enough to be the people who actually help."

Praying for our Church leaders and missionaries is also very important. First of all, these people are immersed in our service and need our prayers. But secondly, children learn to honor and respect them more when they're taught to pray for their strength and their success. They will be more likely to follow the counsel of the prophet if they've learned to love him by praying for him.

Children can also pray for their own futures. They can pray for strength to resist the tremendous temptations that lurk out in the world around them. They can pray for testimonies. They can pray to stay clean and righteous so that they might someday go to the temple. They can pray to be worthy of serving a mission. They can pray for their future husband or wife, that this person will be properly prepared and will be found when the time is right. They can pray about all the choices that shape their destiny—what friends to choose, which fields to study, where to attend college, what jobs to take, where to move, and on and on. Most of our major decisions are made when we are still relatively young, and we need divine guidance.

Children must also be taught to listen to the Holy Ghost and to recognize His voice. This is possibly the greatest gift you can give your children, as it will help in every decision they ever make, especially in the all-important decision about whom to marry.

The Holy Ghost is also He who will testify to your child's heart that God lives, that the Book of Mormon is true, that the Church is Christ's own, and that we are led by a living prophet. When children learn to listen to, and heed, His promptings, they live more joyously, more peacefully, more safely.

As children grow, they stumble over insecurities and weaknesses. (Actually, so do grown-ups.) But children are learning social skills for the first time, experimenting with talents and abilities they've never tried before, discovering their physical limitations, and ultimately learning who they are and what they're meant to do in life. These are times to pray for insight. God can take our darkest trait, our most difficult weakness, and turn it into a strength—if we're willing to work with Him and do our part. In fact, that's one of God's many "Surprise—it's more!" blessings, when He not only helps us conquer a weakness but turns it into one of our greatest strengths.

He can take someone addicted to gambling, turn their heart 180 degrees, and make them a genius at handling finances. He can take a shy person and make them a sought-after public speaker. He can help a smoker become an antitobacco lobbyist. He can turn a slow learner into a gifted musician. He can humble the arrogant, infuse love into a cold heart, make a thief into an honest man, and create heroes out of ordinary people. Like a sculptor working with clay, He can transform us from shapeless lumps into works of art.

All it takes on our part is intense determination and a refusal to give up. Like the clay, we must be pliable in God's hands. We pray for God's help with a righteous change we wish to make, and it is there in abundance. Sometimes it is great pain that leads us to such determination, but once we are resolute, God makes us unstoppable. Look how often He chose leaders who felt utterly inadequate—Moses, who was "slow of speech" (Ex. 4:10); Enos, who felt such a profound desire for repentance (see Enos 1:4)—and made them into spiritual giants. When we are truly repentant and want desperately to serve the Lord, He does wondrous things with us.

Children are not too young to see this at work in their own lives. If a child is struggling with honesty, God can help her become unfailingly honest, a person known for keeping her word. He can take a boy who pursues pornography and make it completely repugnant to him. A child with a terrible temper can learn meekness and self-control. God can help a child who is slow to forgive to see the joy and freedom of forgiving others. He can put confidence where jealousy was, purity where sin was, and kindness where cruelty was. Once children learn to work hand in hand with God to conquer their failings, they will know how to enact miracles, and genuine changes of heart, all their lives.

CHAPTER EIGHT

LEHI'S DREAM AND YOUR PRAYERS

*What you sincerely in your heart think of Christ will determine
what you are, will largely determine what your acts will be.*
—DAVID O. McKAY

Early in the Book of Mormon, we hear about a marvelous
dream. Father Lehi is shown a vision of the tree of life, a scene
which has penetrated people's hearts for centuries. Archaeologists
have found evidence in ruins in Central America that the story of
the tree of life was told anciently. To this day, many cultures in
North and South America continue to tell stories which include a
tree of life, and woven renditions of it hang in many Central
American homes. Lehi's vision of the tree of life contains powerful
insights into prayer. (See 1 Ne. 8.)

Let's recap. An angel wearing a white robe appears to Lehi and
leads him for hours in darkness. It is so oppressive that Lehi prays
to the Lord for mercy. Now he sees a spacious field and a tree
bearing gorgeous, white fruit. Drawn to the fruit, he tastes it and
discovers such intense joy that he calls to his family to partake with
him. Lehi's wife and two of his sons join him, but the eldest,
Laman and Lemuel, will not.

Now Lehi sees that a narrow path and a rod of iron beside a river-
bank lead to the tree. At the other end of the rod is what an angel
later described to Nephi as a "fountain of filthy water" (1 Ne. 12:16)
and a "large and spacious field" (1 Ne. 8:20). In the field, Lehi

observes numerous people trying to get to the tree. They find the path, but a mist of darkness confuses many, who wander off and are lost. Some reach the rod, hold fast, and eventually make it through the mist and to the tree of life.

Lehi looks across the river and sees a huge building in the air, filled with finely dressed people who are scoffing at those who ate the tree's fruit. Their mocking embarrasses some of those who made it all the way, and even though they survived the mist of darkness and tasted the fruit, they now wander off under the derision and chiding of the mockers.

Others feel their way to the great and spacious building. Still others drown in the fountain or take "strange roads" (1 Ne. 8:32) and fall from Lehi's view.

Nephi wants desperately to know the meaning of his father's dream. While pondering alone, he is caught up by the Spirit to a high mountain and shown the same vision. He learns that the tree is the Son of God, and he sees Christ's birth, ministry, and Crucifixion. He realizes that by sending Jesus Christ to atone for our sins, God has given us the greatest gift possible, the most delicious fruit imaginable. By partaking of Christ's atoning sacrifice (repenting and turning our hearts toward God), we will be filled with joy beyond description.

Both Lehi and Nephi preach strenuously the lessons of this vision—they try fervently to get Laman and Lemuel to believe and to understand that obedience to God's word is the only way to reach Christ and exaltation. However, despite hopeful moments of cooperation, the two older brothers eventually fall away.

How does Lehi's dream impact your prayers today?

I attended a Know Your Religion lecture by Max Caldwell some years ago, and I recall him saying that every human falls into one of four groups—the very groups identified in Lehi's vision. First, there are the lost souls who grabbed onto the rod but were overcome by the mists of darkness. These people started out with the right idea but were too weak to press forward with faith and determination. They succumbed to a myriad of sins and temptations, and many of them ended up in the spacious building. The second group is made of people who made it all the way to the tree and even tasted the fruit—but couldn't stand being made fun of by the proud and wealthy. These people care more about what others think of them than about what the Lord thinks.

The next group is Lehi's group—those who made it all the way, ignored the taunts of the world, tasted the brilliant white fruit, and stayed faithful.

And the final group comprises folks who never even took the path. They are wandering in fruitless directions, believing false teachings, and falling prey to the adversary. Many of them have succumbed to the river or the fountain, which represent hell and wickedness.

The entire key to which group you fall into is *what you think of Christ.* And this has everything to do with how you pray, what you pray for, and where you're going. It determines your priorities and whether you place more stock in the approval of the public or the approval of God.

Prayer helps us develop that relationship with Christ, that faith strong enough to keep us holding the rod, even when others scorn us, even when dark mists arise. Obedience despite all obstacles is how we will finally be able to taste the glistening fruit, to know the fullness of joy, to live again with God and His Son.

When you pray, think about where you are in that grand mural of human history—have you stumbled and lost your grip on the iron rod? Are you loosening just a finger or two? Are you fumbling around trying to find your way back? Are you a frequent weekend guest in the great and spacious bed-and-breakfast? Do you have some repenting to do, some recommitting?

Notice how, right after describing his vision, Lehi sought to teach his elder, rebellious sons to repent before it was too late (see 1 Ne. 8:36–38). There is a great message in this for every parent whose children ever disappoint or lose their way, and the message is this: Lehi was a phenomenal parent whose eldest boys still chose evil over good. Those boys, like all our children, had agency and were taught properly but turned away. Your stewardship over your children can still be complete and worthy in God's eyes, even if your children make unwise choices. Notice, too, how Lehi never gave up on them, how he continued to pray for them and try to work with them. When we pray about the frustrations of parenting, we would be wise to remember Father Lehi and the joy and peace he found, despite his mortal heartbreaks. He wasn't sent down into the dirty river as punishment for his sons' mistakes, and you won't be either.

Notice the trials presented in the vision. They are not trials of cold, illness, starvation, or physical danger, such as beset the early pioneers. They are the temptations of luxury and pride. Wanting to "fit in," to be like others in the world, is what ensnares so many in Lehi's vision.

Numerous modern-day prophets have warned us of the dangers of ease and materialism, which is why it is so important to constantly evaluate ourselves and where we are in the scheme of Lehi's vision. It's easy to lose one's grip on the iron rod when so much finery beckons so closely.

It's also easy to label other members' righteous efforts as "fanatic" if we are unwilling to show similar dedication. Scoffing at those who keep the laws we are too weak to embrace puts us firmly in the great and spacious building, not at the base of the tree.

And what about that iron rod? Why is it made of iron instead of being a rope or simply a trail to follow? Iron represents power, immovability, and solid, unwavering strength. God's laws are firm, and only by devoted obedience can we find our way to the tree of life. Holding fast to the rod means *not* treating gospel principles as a smorgasbord of choices, picking here and there which ones we want to obey. No, holding fast means not letting go for anything—not rationalizing or stretching the rules, but adhering "fast," like glue.

Truly, Lehi's vision is a message for all cultures and all times. It's easy to see why this important imagery was passed down through tribes and groups wishing to teach obedience and faith. Artists have portrayed the vision a hundred different ways, and each of us pictures it differently in our minds. But no matter how it is painted or woven into tapestry, the tree of life beckons. Now we must hold fast to the rod and pray always for strength that we might do so.

CHAPTER NINE

UNSPOKEN PRAYERS

Certain thoughts are prayers. There are moments when,
whatever the attitude of the body, the soul is on its knees.
—VICTOR HUGO

Have you ever wondered if a prayer didn't "count" because you weren't kneeling with a bowed head? While it's important to do so when at all possible, and while it shows our reverence for God, there are innumerable times in life when it simply isn't possible, yet our heart cries out to Him for help or comfort.

These prayers are heard also. Have you ever prayed while in traffic, doing chores, sitting in a classroom, taking a walk, attending to your work, ringing the doorbell to visit someone, or working on a project of some kind? The Book of Mormon missionary Amulek teaches us to pray even when we can't vocalize our prayers. "Yea, and when you do not cry unto the Lord, let your hearts be full, drawn out in prayer unto him continually for your welfare, and also for the welfare of those who are around you" (Alma 34:27).

It is good to have a prayer in our hearts at all times and constantly be reaching to God—if only to listen for instruction! It also acknowledges our utter dependence upon Him for everything we have and are in this life. Remembering this is so important that it forms one of the major covenants we make when we partake of the sacrament. It also reminds us of our duty to magnify all He has given us and to make the world better.

In modern revelation the Lord admonished, "Pray always, that ye may not faint, until I come. Behold, and lo, I will come quickly, and receive you unto myself" (D&C 88:126). In other words, don't give up—keep praying to valiantly endure whatever life brings, and stay faithful until Christ sweeps you into His arms and tells you you've finished.

As we embark upon our daily tasks, we must not forget to bring God with us. Nephi taught, "Ye must pray always, and not faint; . . . ye must not perform any thing unto the Lord save in the first place ye shall pray unto the Father in the name of Christ, that he will consecrate thy performance unto thee, that thy performance may be for the welfare of thy soul" (2 Ne. 32:9).

Many times when I have received specific, worded instruction from the Holy Ghost, it has been when I have had the attitude of prayer in my heart. Perhaps I wasn't actually thinking the words of a prayer per se, but I was drawing close, leaning in, and listening intently.

Emergencies also arise in life that do not allow for much preparation. As the rocks of an avalanche are falling, God would understand, I think, if you prayed on the run. It's the same with more common experiences: You drive into a parking lot to pick up your child from high school and you see her talking with an unsavory-looking crowd. A prayer comes immediately to mind. Your toddler has wandered away from the campground. Almost without thinking, you begin to pray. A mugger snatches your wallet. Your angry boss has asked to see you immediately. You hear that a relative has had a stroke. Yes, prayer leaps from our hearts in a whisper or a thought at such times.

And there are times in life when hardships seem so insurmountable that we find ourselves praying a constant prayer, almost all day long, as we fold laundry, as we cook meals, from morning until night. We scarcely seem to finish one prayer before we start up another of earnest pleading. True sorrow can create constant prayer, and so can real repentance.

God also hears our thoughts, and righteous desires can be like prayers. Have you ever heard some bad news about someone and immediately thought, "Oh, I hope they make it through," even before you think to pray for them? This kind wish, this instant desire for their rescue, can rise to heavenly ears, and your righteous hopes can be heard. Father in Heaven knows your heart and knows your sincerest desires. He wants to bring joy to those whose wishes have come into line with His.

Prayer in the workplace or at school is a necessity, and often these prayers must be unspoken. They can still wield great strength. Stories are told of Christians imprisoned in antireligious countries where they have been forbidden by law to pray. And yet they pray in their hearts, and their prayers are heard. This is the art of prayer—to have prayer in your heart at all times, to be reaching out to the Lord to know His will and then do it.

President Joseph F. Smith said, "Is there any one who doubts the ability of God to hear the earnest, honest supplication of the soul? . . . He has means of hearing and understanding your innermost, exact thoughts" (*Gospel Doctrine*, 216).

The question is really, do we hear Him?

CHAPTER TEN

Listening for the Answer

If you are too busy to pray, you are too busy.
—Anonymous

I like to call it "Prayer Plus One." It's taking an extra minute just to listen once you've prayed. We must all step out of the incessant march of worldly time, with its schedules and deadlines and pressures, to pray *and then to listen.* We must resist the urge to jump back on the commuter train and vanish in a blur or to hop right into bed and turn our thoughts to tomorrow's plans or sleep.

We must remember that prayer is a conversation—a two-way conversation. The response may not always come instantly, but it will come. Failing to listen is failing to finish the conversation. As mentioned earlier in this book, you would not appreciate that kind of treatment from a close acquaintance.

After praying, take time to meditate upon your concerns. Block out distractions and really strive to feel in tune with your Father in Heaven. Make time for this, just as you expect God to make time for what *you* have to say.

Sometimes it takes a bit of preparation. Here are some ways to set the stage for listening.

Establish the right environment. Though we aren't always able to control our praying circumstances, as mentioned in the last chapter, we can usually control our daily prayer time (morning and night) and where we kneel to speak to our Father. Take care to select times when you are not rushed or sleepy and places where you can concentrate. You want to give Him your best time, not the leftovers of an exhausting day.

Make sure it's quiet. Don't pray when a TV or radio is blaring in the background, or where raucous laughter is sure to interrupt your thoughts. Even music or the constant ticking of a clock can be enough intrusion into some folks' prayers that it pulls them off track. You may even want to alert family members that you need some quiet time for a while and wish not to be interrupted. Then go where you can be alone and close the door.

Have a plan ready to present if you're in need of specific guidance (see chapter 5). Take time to do whatever research is needed.

Study the scriptures to get focused and to elevate you from the hubbub of daily activities. Seek the companionship of the Holy Ghost as you study and continue to seek it as you pray. Elder Bruce R. McConkie instructed, "Pray by the power of the Holy Ghost. This is the supreme and ultimate achievement in prayer" (*Ensign,* January 1976).

Have faith as you pray, not doubts. Remember that God will answer those who earnestly seek Him. Summon your deepest desires.

Do your part. "Ask, and it shall be given you; seek, and ye shall find; knock, and it shall be opened unto you" (Matt. 7:7). Three times in that scripture we are told that we must take action before God will rush in to answer us. Truly ask, seek, and knock. Don't just kneel, mumble, and rush on. Jeremiah 29:13 tells us, "And ye shall seek me, and find me, when ye shall search for me with all your heart." All your heart! In 2 Nephi 32:4 we read, "Wherefore, now after I have spoken these words, if ye cannot understand them it will be because ye ask not, neither do ye knock; wherefore, ye are not brought into the light, but must perish in the dark." We definitely have to do our part to get answers. Sometimes they come from scripture.

Set aside enough time. Prayers offered as we're dashing out the door may indeed have answers, but we're long gone and cannot hear them! On days when you feel you just don't have time to pray, remember that such a busy day requires God's help, and the truth is that you don't have time *not* to pray.

Be open. When we listen for the answers, we must not allow our favorite choices (or the easiest ones) to dominate our thoughts; rather, we must try earnestly to be open to every possibility. If we're really just begging to be right, we aren't truly listening.

As you quiet your soul and your secret yearnings, as you submit completely to the Father, you might just hear the whisperings of the Holy Ghost. And His voice is unmistakable. It is not a thundering, frightening voice, but a quiet and loving voice that seems to penetrate your mind and heart, overriding anything else you were just thinking. This is the still, small voice that testifies of truth. It tells earnest seekers that Joseph Smith restored the original church Christ established anciently, that the Book of Mormon is an authentic scriptural record, that we have a living prophet today, and that Christ lives and loves us. Those who desire to know that these things are true can pray earnestly and expect to get the answer. This promise is given in the Book of Mormon itself (see Moro. 10:3–5), but I also like to remember Psalms 34:4, which says, "I sought the Lord, and He heard me, and delivered me from all my fears."

Be patient. Not all answers come while you are still on your knees. Sometimes God waits for us to do our part, show our faith, or get into a receptive attitude so we can hear His instructions. Sometimes He has to wait a long time for us to be in a frame of mind where we can even accept an idea different from the one we want.

In fact, there are times when the Holy Ghost suddenly prompts you to do something quite contrary to your existing plans. (Otherwise, if you were already doing the right thing, why would He need to get through to you with a message?) His urgings might even seem illogical or unnecessary, maybe even a little crazy at first. Why should you move your car? Or stand somewhere else for a moment? Or call someone at exactly this instant? Or check again on a sleeping child you just checked on? Believe me, you will find out. If we follow the promptings of the Holy Ghost, we often witness miracles. If we reject or ignore His promptings, we live to grieve and regret our stubbornness and our foolish certainty that we knew better.

Many of the messages given by the power of the Holy Ghost are too sacred and personal in nature to share. But some are less intimate, and I'll give you an example of how the Holy Ghost gets through to us.

I had to drop by the Relief Society president's house one day after a huge rainstorm. The street was still wet, and as I parked and went in, I noticed across the street a large tree that had fallen over. Coming out, I headed to my car but heard the distinct words, "Move the tree." At first, I shook it off—what a crazy idea, right? I wasn't interested in trying to move a huge tree. I was leaving. Again, "Move the tree." This was ridiculous. I was all dressed up! And there was no way one weak woman could budge that huge trunk. The thought was ridiculous. Finally, "Move the tree" echoed through my chest, and I thought, "Okay, fine. You want me to move the tree? Watch. This is not going to work." But I went over to the tree, clasped one of the smaller branches, and tried to lift it. It didn't budge. I pushed on the trunk itself, hoping to roll it an inch or so. Nothing. I threw my whole skinny self into the endeavor, pushing as hard as I could on the tree.

Just then, screeching around the corner came a Jeep with four young men in it. Four husky young men, laughing and swerving to get around the tree. And then they saw me. Here was this woman, all dressed up, trying to move a tree all by herself. Guilt got the better of them, and they stopped to offer help. Within seconds, like a team of professional piano movers, they had scooted the tree to the side of the road, where it would no longer obstruct traffic.

I waved my thanks as they left, then prayed humbly for forgiveness for doubting an inspired message. If I hadn't obeyed the prompting, those fellows very likely would have careened on their happy way and wouldn't have stopped to help. The tree would have stayed there and possibly caused an accident to a less careful driver. I will never know the crisis that was averted by my stopping to do something that seemed, at first, preposterous. I have since learned to listen a bit more carefully.

On another occasion, I was wallowing in self-pity at having turned down a writer/producer position on a television show so that I could spend more time with my children. I prayed about this difficult sacrifice and asked God why I was given my talents if I wasn't to use them. Why did I go out and get a master's degree in professional writing? Why did I have this workaholic streak in me, even from childhood? Wasn't I meant to do other things (and make a fortune)? In the midst of my despair, distinct words cut through my self-made misery: "Don't discount motherhood." Three simple words of chastisement. I had been diminishing the importance of a truly sacred calling. I had taken for granted a blessing and an assignment from God Himself. *Of course* motherhood was more important than writing television episodes! How could I not have seen this more clearly? How could I have wondered about where I could do my best work? (How can God have so much patience, and not reach down to knock us on the head at times and say, "Hello? Hello?") Sometimes revelation is not to save us physically, but spiritually.

Answers to prayers sometimes come in the form of a question. On one occasion I was praying about whether to allow my son to break one of the family's rules. He had made an excellent, logical case for it and had persuaded me that this one exception wouldn't matter in the overall scheme of things.

Just to be sure, I took it to the Lord in prayer. Instantly, I heard the words, "What kind of man are you raising?" And I knew that if I acquiesced to my son, I could raise an ordinary, common man. But if I wanted to raise a leader, a man of God, I had to hold firm to the family's rules. The question was my answer.

When my husband was in the navy, his job was to film every plane landing on his aircraft carrier. Every day he'd stand at a certain spot on the catwalk, where he could get the best shots. One day, as he got into his usual position, he heard a voice tell him to move a few feet to the right. What for? What difference could a few feet make? Again, he was prompted. And again.

He moved. And just then a fighter jet came screeching down toward the flight deck, dropping its tail hook. It missed the first two lines, but caught the third. Thinking he had missed the third line as well, the pilot tried to take off again. In a heartbeat, the pilot realized that the tail hook had caught, and he immediately cut power, causing the plane to slam down onto the deck. The front wheel assembly exploded, sending a burst of shrapnel to the exact spot where my husband normally would have been standing. The lifeboats he usually leaned against were shredded. The flight deck crew rushed over to the plane to see if the pilot was injured and what damage the plane had sustained. They also needed to move it quickly out of the landing area, as other planes were waiting to come in. No one even realized that just a few feet away a miracle had happened.

Even when it doesn't make sense, listen and obey.

CHAPTER ELEVEN

WHEN THE ANSWER IS NO

*The God of heaven would not expect us to pray
to him if he had no intention of answering our prayers.*
—VAUGHN J. FEATHERSTONE

Our mortal perspective is a blessing and, at times, a frustration. It is a blessing because we aren't ready for the obligations of knowing more and being more responsible. Like children, we have been given only as much as we can understand. But it is a frustration because we simply cannot see into the future or know what's best for us in every situation.

Thankfully, there is One who can, and we can turn to Him for guidance. The trick is, we must trust what He tells us. And sometimes, like all parents can testify, the answer has to be no. It may not make sense to us from our limited position, but we must remember that, in a way, we are blindfolded. We cannot see the whole picture any more than the fabled blind men could see the elephant.

Being told no is often painful for children and turns many against their parents. When they cannot have their way, some children throw a tantrum, or storm away and sever ties to the family. With time and maturity, some of these souls see their errors and return. Better yet, some children obey without a quarrel in the first place, even though their parents' answer is not to their liking. Those are the kids who navigate more smoothly, who trust their parents' judgment and eventually see the wisdom of their decisions.

This is the kind of submission we need to give to our Heavenly Father. Even when His answer is no, we need to accept it and trust that He knows something we don't. This becomes difficult when we lose a loved one in death or when other tragedies strike. We find it hard to understand how a loving God can allow entire villages to be swept away or small children to suffer. We forget that we are on a field trip and that we're here to learn. This life is not our permanent state—separation from those we love will end at death when we rejoin them in the hereafter. And those who have suffered will be at peace, their suffering in righteousness counted to them for blessings. By enduring afflictions, we grow and develop the traits we will need in the hereafter. It's the whole reason we came to Earth. We all knew we were in for a roller coaster ride, so it hardly makes sense to beg for a seat and then complain that there are too many ups and downs.

President Kimball gave a wonderful explanation for why we sometimes get no for an answer.

> We find many people critical when a righteous person is killed, a young father or mother is taken from a family, or when violent deaths occur. Some become bitter when oft-repeated prayers seem unanswered. Some lose faith and turn sour when solemn administrations by holy men seem to be ignored and no restoration seems to come from repeated prayer circles. But if all the sick were healed, if all the righteous were protected and the wicked destroyed, the whole program of the Father would be annulled and the basic principle of the gospel, free agency, would be ended.

> If pain and sorrow and total punishment immediately followed the doing of evil, no soul would repeat a misdeed. If joy and peace and rewards were instantaneously given the doer of good, there could be no evil—all would do good and not because of the rightness of doing good. There

would be no test of strength, no development of character, no growth of powers, no free agency, no satanic controls.

Should all prayers be immediately answered according to our selfish desires and our limited understanding, then there would be little or no suffering, sorrow, disappointment, or even death; and if these were not, there would also be an absence of joy, success, resurrection, eternal life, and godhood. (*Improvement Era,* March 1966)

We must not only accept no for an answer, but sometimes we must submit ourselves to the chastisement and instruction of God. He does not sit on high hurling bolts of lightning into our paths, but He does allow trials in our lives, that we might be tested and learn. He allows natural consequences to befall us when we choose to sin, and He even allows us to see that one person's actions can affect others.

Occasionally, God even grants us things we pray for that are not for our best, so He can teach us. The phrase, "Be careful what you ask for; you just might get it," is often true when we pursue mistaken paths and find that the success we thought we wanted ultimately rings hollow.

Conversely, by submitting our will to His, we show that we are willing to trade our own finite knowledge for His infinite knowledge. We take that leap of faith, we show we are willing to risk our own view for the unknown, and the Lord grants us amazing opportunities that we couldn't have imagined on our own. But we have to be willing to hear no.

Many times we assume that our prayers are not answered, when the answer is really "not yet." We want everything to happen immediately and forget that God has His own timetable. When we are praying for a righteous cause, we must exercise patience as well as faith, and trust that He will choose the right time for the best outcome.

A perfect example of this is when we try to pray away someone else's agency. We pray for a wayward child to return, or for someone to make wiser choices, or for a loved one to join the Church. What we want in our hearts is a noble, righteous thing, and we can't imagine why the Lord wouldn't agree with us and just *make it happen* the way He created the heavens and the earth. We sometimes forget that one of His most cherished laws is freedom to choose for oneself—it's how we got here, how the plan of salvation works, and how we become exalted. We fought a war for it! We cannot pray for a pause button in that holy plan. We *can* pray for opportunities to come along for those we love, for teaching moments to present themselves, for our own influence to be loving rather than nagging, and for hearts to be softened. But we cannot take over another person's mental function and choose for them. It goes contrary to God's ways. Believe me, I know this is frustrating, and, like many members, I have joked that I'm for agency for everybody except my own children. But it is nevertheless an immutable law, and you waste your breath when you try to pray it away. These are the times when we can fully expect the answer no.

When you do hear the answer no, try something that turns the event into a positive experience. Try to learn from that answer. Why did God say no? What could be the possible reasons? Really think outside the box and try to be the parent answering the child's question. Might there be something unseen that could justify a negative answer? If you really open your heart up to the possibilities, you will learn something. You might even be granted enough foresight to realize how foolish it would be to be given your desires.

Look for the lesson in it. How can you take what seems to be a setback and help others with it? How can terrible predicaments be used to better the world? How can we reach outside the bubble of our own selves? I'm not saying it's easy, but consider what you can do with "no" answers to the following.

Your cancer will not be cured. You can work with others to help them face their futures, get their lives in order, and gain the testimonies they need before it's too late. You can mend fences and repent. You can learn to forgive and let go of old grudges and feel freer and lighter than you've ever felt before. You can know God.

You will not get the job you applied for. You will have to go in another direction, which will turn out even better. You may learn humility at first. You will be guided to a lifelong friend. You will set an example for a relative who needs your time. You will be put in a position of Church leadership that would have been impossible the other way.

You won't get into the college you've always wanted. You will meet your future spouse at another college. You will meet a professor who introduces you to your life's passion. You will have to work harder to reach your goals and thus develop a dozen traits essential to a happy life.

You will not marry. You will find yourself serving as a volunteer in the slums of a foreign country and will find joy and satisfaction beyond your wildest dreams. You will devote yourself to the children in an orphanage. You will spend your time in research and discover the cure for a disease. You will accept a job that requires constant travel but blesses the lives of millions. You will be compared to Mother Teresa.

The point is, *who knows?* Only God knows what the future holds for you, and to reach your full potential you might have to hear no when you stray from the right path. Remember, there can be several seemingly right choices, but only God knows the best one. So, when it seems you are directed away from a perfectly fine choice, have faith that an even better one awaits.

"Lean not unto thine own understanding" (Prov. 3:5).

Joseph Smith said, "The best way to obtain truth and wisdom is not to ask it from books, but to go to God in prayer, and obtain divine teaching" (*Teachings of the Prophet Joseph Smith*, 191). A big part of teaching is redirecting when the student goes the wrong way. "No" has to be part of the learning process.

Sometimes our prayers are ineffective not because God isn't listening, but because we aren't exercising faith or living the way we know we should. There are dozens of "prayer blockers" we all employ from time to time: distractions while praying, getting lost in a mire of set phrases, asking for easy ways out of problems we created, expecting blessings when we haven't done our part, praying when we're too sleepy to pay attention, and the worst of all—sin. If we are not doing our best, repenting regularly, and really trying to improve, we cannot expect God to come running to our aid. If we are giving in to wickedness, pride, lustful desires, selfishness, cruelty, or any other temptation, we have no claim upon divine assistance. As it says in Isaiah 59:2, "Your sins have hid His face from you, that He will not hear."

Sin acts like a tourniquet on our testimonies, choking them off and discouraging us from prayer and growth. As President Brigham Young stated, "Prayer keeps a man from sin, and sin keeps a man from prayer" (cited in *Tambuli,* August 1983). If you feel hesitant to pray, look into your life for prayer blockers, and reopen the channel of communication.

Sometimes what we pray for is against God's will. I was privileged to know a descendant of Joseph Knight's some time ago, and though we were fifty years apart in age, we became good friends. Ardella was bedridden the entire time I knew her, and when her health took a turn for the worse, she was hospitalized. Like many, I prayed for her recovery. I remembered holding her cream-colored hands and stroking her thin, silver hair as I begged her not to die. But she knew better. "I wish you'd all stop praying for me and keeping me here," she finally snapped. I smiled. She was right. It was her time, and we needed to pray for the strength to let her go, not for God's will to be circumvented.

When my cousin Barbara was diagnosed with a cancerous brain tumor, you would have thought she'd won a million dollars. I have never in my life spoken to anyone more upbeat about having a terminal illness. All she could see were the positive outcomes: She finally got sealed to her husband. Her daughter went to the temple for the first time. Family members who had been disconnected were connecting again. All Barbara could see was a joyous gathering in of loved ones, an explosion of testimony building, a fulfilling of promises made long ago, and a gloriously happy ending.

"You actually sound excited," I said during one of our last phone calls.

"I *am!*" she responded. "You should see me in my bandages—I look like a conehead, but I've never been so thrilled. I'd go through this all over again, if this could be the result!" Her funeral was a celebration of light and right—here was a woman whose example set the bar a little higher for the rest of us. She took God at His word and allowed His majesty to direct her destiny. She never lost faith, never gave up hope, never stopped learning from the no's. Instead of praying to get well, she allowed herself to be the instrument of miracles. God kept His promises to her and answered her most fervent prayers with a resounding "Yes!" Something tells me that she won't just hear, "Well done," on the other side, but perhaps, "Spectacularly done!" Thank you, Barbara. You changed the way I pray.

CHAPTER TWELVE

PRAYERS OF REPENTANCE

*If ye will repent and harden not your hearts, immediately
shall the great plan of redemption be brought about unto you.*
—ALMA 34:31

Probably the most important prayer you will ever pray is the one for forgiveness. Without it, you cannot partake of the full blessings of Christ's Atonement in your life. You cannot progress; you cannot attain "all that [the] Father hath" (D&C 84:38).

Throughout time, prophets old and new have admonished us to repent, to confess our sins to God, and to beg for His mercy in order to be forgiven. "Say nothing but repentance unto this generation" (D&C 6:9; 11:9).

If we keep our repentance up to date, then we can partake of Christ's ultimate gift—His payment for our sins, which makes them as if they are no more. If we have endured valiantly, we can hope to attain the celestial kingdom, where we will live in an exalted state.

On the other hand, if we procrastinate our repentance, then we have to pay and suffer for those errors in the next life ourselves. The Atonement is not enacted in our behalf. We forfeit the power of the Lord's incredible, priceless sacrifice. Yes, we all still get resurrected. But our sins will go with us if we have not repented of them. This is what Alma was trying to spare his people when he expressed the hope that they "may not suffer the second death" (Alma 13:30).

Repentance is one of the most misunderstood principles in the gospel. Because it is essential for your exaltation, Satan has done an excellent job of blurring what is known and thought about repentance. Many think repentance is accomplished with a simple "I'm sorry" during prayer (whether they mean it or not). Others think repentance is complete when a set amount of time has passed since the sin was committed. Still others think they have repented if their transgressions have caused them pain and suffering.

All of those ideas are wrong. Simply praying "I'm sorry" does not always reflect what we honestly feel inside, and it certainly does nothing to repair damage or make amends to those we may have hurt. Telling God you're sorry when you're still justifying why you did it is ridiculous. So is blaming someone else for it or thinking it wasn't so bad after all. Heavenly Father knows exactly how you feel about the misdeed and whether your regret is complete or partial. Even if you're really sorry, you need to demonstrate changed behavior and strength when temptation strikes again. This is why deathbed repentance is impossible; you have no opportunity to really show a changed heart. In fact, if you wait until then, you "become subjected to the spirit of the devil, and he doth seal you his" (Alma 34:35).

"Waiting out your time" is also a myth. You can't commit a crime, then cease and desist for six months or a year and expect to feel, or be, forgiven. Many folks think it's harsh when disciplined members are not reinstated after a year, and they feel they've already "paid their price." But sins are not washed away by marking off days on a calendar or by setting an alarm clock or by reaching a certain age. You wouldn't expect to pay money for forgiveness; likewise, you cannot pay with time. You must make changes in the hardwiring of your brain, not just hang your head until time's up.

Mere suffering, though it can be sore and agonizing, is not repentance either. Many of us stumble and cause ourselves pain in this life. But if we don't learn from the experience, if we don't make needed changes, we're just somebody enduring a lot of suffering.

Thousands of people experience agony due to their poor choices, but they plan to go right out and continue making those poor choices. This is why we cannot say, "He's suffered enough," about a repenting person. He may go on suffering for the rest of his life if he never turns his soul around. It's painful to watch, but pain alone cannot quicken the renewal of one's spirit if the person doesn't really want to forsake his sins.

So what does it mean, then, to truly repent? King Benjamin's people described it as having "wrought a mighty change in us, or in our hearts, that we have no more disposition to do evil, but to do good continually" (Mosiah 5:2). It means your whole attitude has changed and you have a purified heart. You haven't just stopped shoplifting or gambling or carousing—you have completely removed the very desire from your being. Even the thought of participating in the sin is repugnant to you, and you are appalled that you could ever have once embraced something so repulsive. You become a different person, reborn, dedicated to God and free from being drawn back into that mistake. Your weakness has been turned inside out and has become one of your greatest strengths.

It is not enough merely to *resist* evil, to steel yourself from sin the way an alcoholic refuses a drink. (Or the way some of us feel we can finally diet if the goodies aren't in the house.) To truly repent, you overcome the very temptation—you truly conquer self and master your desires.

Now, let me say that this process is not an easy one, and not everyone who wishes he or she were stronger puts forth the effort and commitment to actually make it happen. But it is possible, and it is worth every moment of anguish and exertion you can muster. It requires tremendous humility, absolute honesty, and the kind of genuine misery that motivates you to work harder than you've ever worked to remake yourself. Fortunately, you have someone who is very invested in your success and will more than match your every investment—you will be working as a teammate with the Savior Himself.

Prayers of real repentance require us to bare our souls to God, often a tearful experience that consumes our every waking thought. These prayers come from deep within our darkest corners and beg for light. Praying for repentance must be done privately, as you are asking for a personal forgiveness, not "group forgiveness." Such prayers can be as long as required to adequately express your feelings and to plead for help. Sometimes a person going through repentance will pray off and on all day and all night. The process can take weeks, months, even years in some cases. It can be an excruciating, draining ordeal, at the same time that it is filled with joy and indescribable love.

The longer we carry our bag of sins, the more comfortable we become with it and the harder it is to empty, even if someone tells us that the Savior will help us. Longtime habits take longer to break than new ones, and this is why it's so critical to get an early start on the endeavor, before the task looks insurmountable.

Repenting of serious sins should involve confession to your bishop as well. He represents the Church, and he can tell you if your mistakes require a council to decide if you need extra help. Please see it that way. It is not wrist slapping or finger wagging. It is loving discipline to help you get back on the right path and back to your Heavenly Father. Just remember that whatever it takes, it's worth it. Your exaltation, your closeness to the Lord, your sense that He has again claimed you as one of His, is worth any amount of embarrassment, shame, guilt, or torment you can imagine. (Christ already suffered that and more for you personally.)

Smaller mistakes need to be repented of on an ongoing basis, which is why we take the sacrament each week. We renew our baptism promises, and we are washed clean again, with a brand new slate and a brand new week ahead of us. If we carry a grudge, speak harshly, judge unfairly, take credit for something we didn't do, or rejoice in someone's failure, these are the kinds of things we need to repent of in our daily prayers. We need to feel genuine remorse, confess our errors to the Lord, pray for His forgiveness, and beg Him to grant us greater strength so that we may not repeat them.

As humans, we make mistakes almost constantly, but we can forsake many of them as we strive to live honestly, admit our weaknesses, love others, and really improve. To forgive an enemy and finally let go of the wounds we've been nursing along is to have a changed heart. To summon patience, and even humor, with someone who continually antagonizes you is to have a changed heart. To give back the extra change when you've always kept it before is to have a changed heart. To put aside laziness or self-indulgence to serve another is to have a changed heart. Each of these personal victories brings you one step closer to the tree of life.

Sometimes the toughest part of repenting is forgiving yourself. Once you've experienced the horror and anguish you feel when you hurt another, it's hard to erase that shame from your mind. Even if the person has forgiven you, and even if you think God has forgiven you, there's still the nagging shame, the guilty suspicion that you've blown it permanently, that you'll never quite enjoy life again and never feel truly deserving of a blessing. What you did was too terrible ever to forget. You can never look that person in the eye again. You can never face your congregation, your relatives, your neighbors. Whenever you sense these creeping feelings of utter despair, here is something for you to remember: Satan is behind that. He absolutely is. He wants you to feel so horrible that you give up entirely, despise yourself, and have no hope for the future whatsoever.

Our loving Heavenly Father, on the other hand, is a God of forgiveness, newness, mercy, and hope. He would never want you to give up. His hand is outstretched to the discouraged at every moment, just waiting for us to reach back and return. None of us need ever feel that we are too wretched, too far gone, for the God of the very universe to help. He has worked miracles with worse sinners than you, and He can certainly help you.

So how do you know when God has accepted your repentance? In Mosiah 4:3 we learn that receiving "a remission of [our] sins" goes hand in hand with "having peace of conscience." And this is your answer. When God has forgiven you, you'll feel it. The Holy Ghost will return to speak with you, to warm your heart, and to fill your soul with peace. That peace is your prison door swinging open, inviting you into a lush meadow where your Savior awaits to greet the new soul you have brought Him.

Satan has packaged repentance as a negative thing—bothersome, uncomfortable, painful, shameful, probably impossible anyway, and definitely something to avoid if you want to be happy. As usual, he has it exactly backwards.

Repentance is not shameful. It's beautiful, it's amazing, and it's a true gift from God. This is a time for rejoicing! Finally, you are on the right track, working and taking action to set things straight. You have reached out to God, and He is helping you forsake the sins that really would trap you in pain and shame—permanently. You are turning the tide of the battle with Satan and heading straight for victory. You are conquering evil, sending Satan back where he came from, and working toward something he'll never have—exaltation with your Father in Heaven.

CHAPTER THIRTEEN

PRAYER AND FASTING

*I have fasted and prayed many days that I might know
these things of myself.*
—ALMA 5:46

Fasting is actually feasting. There is so much more to it than just skipping meals, and it can truly pack your prayers with power and pump insight into your mind. Once a month we abstain from food and drink for twenty-four hours and donate the amount saved (or more if we choose) to assist the poor. This is a beautiful and important part of our monthly fast, and we'll take a closer look at this aspect later in the chapter.

But first, I want to explain what fasting actually does. Fasting has ancient roots and has, from the beginning of time, held an amazing power to expedite, if you will, your prayers. It elevates you from mortal concerns and appetites and pulls you to a higher spiritual plane. Your communication with God is purer, less tied to the elements of mortal life. You can forget about feeding your body and focus upon feeding your soul. You increase your faith, and you demonstrate to God your seriousness in the matters you're praying about.

Helaman 3:35 explains the changes we can experience when we fast sincerely. "They did fast and pray oft, and did wax stronger and stronger in their humility, and firmer and firmer in the faith of Christ, unto the filling their souls with joy and consolation, yea, even to the purifying and the sanctification of their hearts, which sanctification cometh because of their yielding their hearts unto God."

Fasting can also open our minds to greater knowledge and teach us things we can't learn any other way. When Alma was preaching repentance, he assured the people that he knew firsthand what he was talking about: "Behold, I say unto you [these things] are made known unto me by the Holy Spirit of God. Behold, I have fasted and prayed many days that I might know these things of myself" (Alma 5:46).

And we can do the same. We can fast that we might know things of a surety for ourselves. A beautiful promise is found in the Doctrine and Covenants: "If thou shalt ask, thou shalt receive revelation upon revelation, knowledge upon knowledge, that thou mayest know the mysteries and peaceable things—that which bringeth joy, that which bringeth life eternal" (D&C 42:61).

What if you can't fast for health reasons? Are you denied the blessings that come to those who fast? Not at all. The spirit of fasting can be in your heart—the true willingness to fast if only you could and the generosity in giving to the poor. President Joseph F. Smith said, "Better to teach [little children] the principle [of the fast], and then let them observe it when they are old enough to choose intelligently than to so compel them" (*Gospel Doctrine*, 243–44). That way, they will appreciate and love the opportunity, not simply dread a day of going without.

Fasting should have a purpose and should begin and end with prayer. If you have nothing to fast for, have a fast of thanks that life is so filled with blessings at this time. Or fast for someone you know who needs extra comfort or insight at this time. Entire congregations have witnessed the power of everyone fasting together in behalf of one member who is gravely ill, for example. Fasting prior to temple attendance heightens the effectiveness of the experience and the inspiration received there. Fasting before a patriarchal blessing, a temple dedication, and other important events is also appropriate, in addition to our monthly fasts.

I recently attended a temple dedication, via satellite, in our stake center. I had been rushing to get there in time and herding my children, quietly but quickly. I did not bring an especially strong spirit along as I hurried into the chapel. But within just a few feet, I felt something wash over me like a wave. I was physically walking into, and being enveloped by, a wall of the Spirit. It was so strong that it changed the very air around me and even the crispness of my vision. I could tangibly feel an immense level of energy and love permeating the chapel. It was as if my own spirit was blending with this ethereal light, lifting away from my body, and being every-where at once in the room. Instantly, it was made known to me that this richness of Spirit was due to the fasting of so many of my brothers and sisters in that room. Fasting had created a palpable difference that I've never experienced in that room before or since. It moved me immediately to tears of gratitude and tremendous love for all those who had created it by fasting that day.

The veil can be very thin at times, and fasting makes it more so. The sons of Mosiah, who were with Alma the Younger when the angel appeared, were able to preach the gospel among their enemies with much success, in part because they knew the power of fasting. "They had given themselves to much prayer, and fasting; therefore they had the spirit of prophecy, and the spirit of revelation, and when they taught, they taught with power and authority of God" (Alma 17:3).

In fact, when Alma was overcome by the visit of an angel, he regained his voice and strength only after two days of prayer *and fasting* by his father and the priests (see Mosiah 27:22–23).

Disciples of Christ in the Americas were journeying and preaching when they "were gathered together and were united in mighty prayer and fasting" (3 Ne. 27:1). It is then that Christ appeared unto them and asked them what they desired.

Even before visiting the Americas, Christ taught the power of fasting and told His followers that some miracles were performed only "by prayer and fasting" (Matt. 17:20–21).

Truly there can be no question that the act of fasting does something miraculous to empower us, bring us closer to God, and make us better tools in His hands.

Even in Old Testament times, prophets taught their people to fast, particularly in cases of mourning and death, as well as to petition the Lord. Moses fasted while he received the Ten Commandments (see Deut. 9:9; 1 Kgs. 19:8), Esther fasted to save her people (see Esth. 4:16), and countless other great leaders fasted for many days when seeking the Lord's help. Even Christ fasted in the wilderness as He communed with His Father (see Matt. 4:2). Isn't it interesting how many biblical writers, as well as record keepers from other dispensations, included accounts of fasting and the power it generated? The ancients obviously knew this was a great force within man's hands, and they were careful to include it in their writings.

Isaiah explains that fasting is not just a day of sackcloth and ashes when we are to forsake eating. Though fasting can bring us spiritual strength, its central purpose is to help the poor and feed the hungry. Beautiful promises are given if "thou draw out thy soul to the hungry" and keep the law of the fast by donating to those in need. (See Isa. 58:3–12.)

When we fast each month and do not give fast offerings, we're just skipping meals. We have not embraced the true spirit of the law, and we have even done something far more serious: we have robbed the Lord. Malachi 3:8 says, "Will a man rob God? Yet ye have robbed me. But ye say, Wherein have we robbed thee? In tithes and offerings." Taking care of the poor is vital to our salvation—we cannot hope to ignore this counsel and be welcomed back into God's presence with open arms. Fasting once a month is an opportunity to give, and give generously. The Church is noted not only for the millions of dollars it donates worldwide to philanthropic and humanitarian efforts, but for the tender, individual care members receive through the Church welfare program when hard times hit here at home. By contributing a generous fast offering, you ensure that good, hard-working people will retain their dignity as they work for staples and goods supplied to them by the Church.

How wonderful that God instituted a plan for those willing to pay the price, to come so close to Him we can nearly feel His breath. Fasting truly elevates us and provides a spiritual feast. But it becomes nearly celestial when we remember to help the poor at the same time. By lifting others, we lift ourselves.

CHAPTER FOURTEEN

THY WILL BE DONE

O my Father, if it be possible, let this cup pass from me: nevertheless not as I will, but as thou wilt.
—MATTHEW 26:39

Few passages of scripture are as wrenching and poignant as this prayer from Jesus to His Father that the terrible pain and suffering He was enduring could somehow be averted. By means we cannot fathom as mortals, the Savior atoned for the sins of every single child of God who ever lived or would live. He took upon Himself burdens beyond the worst anguish and misery known to man. Later, He told Peter that He had accepted and would indeed drink from the cup (see John 18:11). His willing sacrifice was the ultimate example of perfect submission to the Father.

And then we look at our lives. Now and again, hailstorms of adversity come into our lives, and we wonder if anyone exists upon the earth who has been asked to endure such torment. This is when we need to reread the scriptural accounts of Jesus' suffering. He endured all our pains in the Garden of Gethsemane, not because of any sin on His part, but because He loved us.

Next time you feel crushed by the sorrows of life, turn to the story of Jesus and know that, despite pain so strong that it caused Him to bleed at every pore, He never gave up.

I've had discouraging, devastating moments when I've thought, "Surely this is more than I can bear—God will rescue me and take me home, or He will remove this terrible plight." But He didn't. It was part of my education, and the school of suffering is one of the finest teaching institutions in the world—if we allow ourselves to learn from it. Despair and hopelessness beckon, but we must persevere. We must pray to God for the strength we need to meet the challenges that roll upon us in sequence, almost like the tides of the sea.

Remember what the Lord told Joseph Smith in Liberty Jail: "My son, peace be unto thy soul; thine adversity and thine afflictions shall be but a small moment; And then, if thou endure it well, God shall exalt thee on high; thou shalt triumph over all thy foes" (D&C 121:7–8).

Remember, too, not to give in to self-pity or think your case is extraordinary. Even "if the very jaws of hell shall gape open the mouth wide after thee, know thou, my son, that all these things shall give thee experience, and shall be for thy good. The Son of Man hath descended below them all. Art thou greater than he?" (D&C 122:7–8).

We cannot expect to be exalted without sacrifice and suffering. Sometimes we need to accept the cup and let God know we are willing to endure it all. Abraham was brought to the brink of sacrificing his only son, to teach Abraham what he was made of, and to remind the children of Israel of the coming sacrifice God would make of His Only Begotten Son. Surely Abraham gladly would have had that cup pass from him, but he followed through with prompt obedience and godlike faith.

When sore trials afflict us and we think we simply cannot go on, these are the times we need to let go and tell God in prayer, "Thy will be done." Complete submission to the Lord is really the only pathway to peace and comfort. We must stop fighting against what must be and learn to accept God's will. Doing so will spare us the confusion and bitterness which often beset those who cannot relinquish control, those who refuse to see it any way but their own. In time, we will come to see that God was, as usual, absolutely right. There was a greater purpose we couldn't see, and lessons we needed to learn.

Sometimes we need to remember the purpose of this life. The adversary has twisted many of society's priorities, and we can get swept into thinking that life is about earning money, climbing the social ladder, indulging passions, being popular, and being free from all discomfort. Those things actually have nothing to do with the real meaning of life. In fact, if those things are your goal, you can be pretty sure you are doing something wrong. People who adhere to the Lord's standards are often *not* popular in the world (remember the great and spacious building filled with mockers?). Nor are they obsessed with becoming wealthy, as are those who devote their entire beings to money. And the real followers of Christ are too busy serving others to become full-time pleasure seekers. Last, we are often *un*comfortable because that's how we grow and learn. Life wasn't designed just to be fun and easy. When we bemoan our setbacks, we are showing lack of understanding about why we're here in the first place. We are supposed to rise to the occasion when trouble hits and show our Coach how we play the game. Bench warming is not the idea.

One of the lessons of this life is to accept God's will and be able to pray for it sincerely. When we are told that God made man to have joy, that doesn't mean momentary laughs or entertainment. It means the deep, fulfilling joy that comes from knowing Christ and striving to please Him. It comes from enduring trials and gaining character traits such as humility and genuine love for your fellow man. It comes from putting your whole trust in God and letting Him know it.

"Thy will be done" refers to God's will for you eternally. And what is His ultimate will? His will is that you endure well, serve and love others, repent, and obey Him so He can exalt you and bring you all the way home someday.

My prayer is that every one of us will.

SOURCES CITED

Chapter 1
Twain, Mark. *The Adventures of Huckleberry Finn.* New York: The New American Library, 1959.

Chapter 2
McConkie, Bruce R. *Mormon Doctrine.* 2nd ed. Salt Lake City: Bookcraft, 1966.

Chapter 3
Shakespeare, William. *Hamlet.*

Chapter 4
Robinson, E. A. *Collected Poems of Edwin Arlington Robinson.* New York: Macmillan, 1961.

Chapter 6
Ashton, Marvin J. *Prayer.* Salt Lake City: Deseret Book, 1977.
Mead, Frank S., ed. *Twelve Thousand Inspirational Quotations.* Springfield, MA: Federal Street Press, 2000.
Tennyson, Alfred. *Idylls of the King.* New York: Macmillan, 1907.

Chapter 7
Smith, Joseph F. *Millennial Star,* 25 October 1906, 674.

Chapter 8
McKay, David O. Conference Report, April 1951, 93.

Chapter 9
Hugo, Victor. *Les Misérables.* New York: Penguin, 1987.
Widtsoe, John A., ed. *Gospel Doctrine: Selections from the Sermons and Writings of Joseph F. Smith.* Salt Lake City: Deseret Book, 1939.

Chapter 10
McConkie, Bruce R. "Why the Lord Ordained Prayer." *Ensign,* January 1976.

Chapter 11
Featherstone, Vaughn J. "Thanksgiving Prayer." *New Era,* November 1985.
Kimball, Spencer W. "Tragedy or Destiny." *Improvement Era,* March 1966.
Smith, Joseph. *Teachings of the Prophet Joseph Smith.* Salt Lake City: Deseret Book, 1976.
Young, Brigham. Cited in "Quotations." *Tambuli,* August 1983.

Chapter 13
Widtsoe, John A., ed. *Gospel Doctrine: Selections from the Sermons and Writings of Joseph F. Smith.* Salt Lake City: Deseret Book, 1939.

About the Author

Joni Hilton is the author of fifteen books, many published for the LDS market. She holds a master of fine arts degree in professional writing from USC, is an award-winning playwright, and is frequently published in major magazines. She is a weekly columnist for *Meridian* magazine (an online magazine for LDS readers) and is a writer for *Music and the Spoken Word*. A former TV talk show host in Los Angeles, Joni also travels to major TV markets as a spokesperson for various corporations. She has served as ward Relief Society president, first counselor in a stake Relief Society presidency, and currently serves as regional media consultant in the Sacramento Area where she lives. Many of her motivational-speaking tapes are also released by Covenant. She is married to Bob Hilton, and they are the parents of four children.